EZRA POUND

STUDY NOTES FOR OIB
(L'option internationale du Baccalauréat)

CHRIS WEBSTER

———

ISBN-13: 978-1542902984
ISBN-10: 1542902983

The cover design is based on a portrait of Ezra Pound by John Wyndham.

DEDICATION

To the students in my OIB class 2017-19. The poems of Ezra pound made a great impression on me as a young poet, and I hope that they will inspire you in a similar way.

CONTENTS

Introduction	1
Biography	2
Portrait d'une femme	3
The Seafarer	13
The Garden	25
Salutation	28
Salutation the Second	30
Commission	35
The Bath Tub	40
In a Station of the Metro	43
The River-Merchant's Wife: a Letter	47
Lament of the Frontier Guard	55
The City of Choan	59
Hugh Selwyn Mauberley (parts IV and V)	62
Canto I	72
Canto CXVI	85
Themes	96
Style	103
Pound's Advice to Poets	109
Examination Questions	113
Write Your Own Canto	117
Georgian Poetry	123
Haiku	127

FROM CANTO LXXXI

"You will find" said old André Spire,
that every man on that board (Crédit Agricole)
has a brother-in-law
"You the one, I the few"
said John Adams
speaking of fears in the abstract
to his volatile friend Mr Jefferson.
(To break the pentameter, that was the first heave)
or as Jo Bard says: they never speak to each other,
if it is baker and concierge visibly
it is La Rouchefoucauld and de Maintenon audibly.

INTRODUCTION

These study notes were written for the OIB (L'option Internationale du Baccalauréat) syllabus. They include a Biography, questions on the poems, commentaries sample examination questions, short essays on themes and styles, as well as several "extras". The full text of all the set poems is included for convenience, though it is recommended that students work from the edition recommended in the OIB Text Grids for 2018 and 2019.

The study notes are suitable for both individual and class use. When used in class, one approach would be read the poem with the students then ask them to work through the questions in pairs or small groups. When they have finished, discuss their responses. Only then should the commentaries be read and discussed. On occasions students could be asked to follow up the lesson with different kinds of writing. Sometimes this will be a response to some or all of the questions. Sometimes they could be asked to write their own commentary on a poem (without reading the commentary in the book).

The essay and examination questions at the end of the book can be used in a number of ways: students could be asked to present an essay topic to the class, for example, in a PowerPoint presentation. They can also be used for homework essays and practice under examination conditions.

BIOGRAPHY

Ezra Weston Loomis Pound, born on October 30, 1885. He was the only child of Homer Loomis Pound and Isabel Weston. In 1889 his family moved to Wyncote, Philadelphia. At the age of 15 he told his parents that he wanted to be a poet. He was educated at Cheltenham Military Academy and, in 1901, was admitted to the University of Pennsylvania's College of Liberal Arts. He wrote later on (in 1913) that he resolved that at thirty he would know more about poetry than any man living. It was here that he met Hilda Doolittle, who later went with Pound to London and became involved in the Imagism movement.

Pound graduated with an MA degree in 1906, and got a job as a teacher of Romance languages at Wabash College, but he was dismissed in 1908 for bad behaviour which included smoking cigarillos in the corridor and entertaining women friends in his apartment. He left in 1908 and went to London.

He found that London was "the place for poesy", and having persuaded a bookseller to display his self-published book *A Lume Spento*, soon began to make an impression on the London literary scene.

In 1909, Pound met Dorothy Shakespear at a literary salon (they married in 1914) and through her mother, Olivia, was introduced to William Butler Yeats, whom Pound regarded as the greatest living poet. In June of that year he published a collection of poetry entitled *Personae* which was favourably reviewed and enjoyed commercial success.

Hilda Doolittle arrived in London in May 1911, and with the help and inspiration of others, began to develop the movement known as Imagism. An important influence was Laurence Binyon who introduced Pound to Japanese poetry. At that time, he was working on his next collection, which was published as *Ripostes** (1912), and attempting to apply Imagist principles to his poems.

In 1913, the widow of Ernest Fenollosa, an American who had taught in Japan, gave him her late husband's unpublished notes. Pound was impressed by the rough translations of Chinese poetry and decided to rework them in his own style. These were published in a book entitled *Cathay* (1915).

In 1914 he married Dorothy, despite her parents' concerns about his modest income. During this period he wrote for Wyndham Lewis' literary magazine, *Blast*, which was advertised as covering "Cubism, Futurism, Imagism and all Vital Forms of Modern Art". Imagism was by that time becoming a major literary movement, but Pound was already beginning to move on to experiment with different forms of modernism, as can be seen in the poems in his next publication, *Lustra* (1916).

The First World War had a tremendous psychological effect on Pound. For him, as for many others, it shattered his belief in western civilisation and culture. During this period, he wrote *Hugh Selwyn Mauberley* (published in 1920), a semi-autobiographical poem which includes passages of bitter criticism of the war. As a result of his disillusionment, he left London for Paris in 1921.

It was in Paris that he met the 26-year-old violinist, Olga Rudge, who became his mistress. However, his wife, Dorothy was unhappy in Paris, and so in 1924, the couple moved to Rapallo in Italy. Olga, who was pregnant with Pound's child, followed them, and later gave birth to a daughter whom she named Mary. When Dorothy found out about it, she went on an extended trip to Egypt. Soon after she came back she gave birth to a son, whom they named Omar Pound.

During this period, Pound had returned to his work on **The Cantos**, the first of which had been published in 1917. However, he abandoned his earlier work, and started again. Pound was working on **The Cantos**, which he considered to be his major work, from 1917-1962, though the Cantos written before 1922 were rejected.

In 1933 Pound met Benito Mussolini and this reinforced his idea that the main cause of the First World War was the finance system, which he called "usury". This idea was unfortunately linked with anti-Semitism. He believed that the Second World War was the result of an international banking conspiracy and urged, in a series of letters, that the United States should keep out of it. During the 1940's he gave a series of radio broadcasts praising Mussolini and Fascism and criticising Roosevelt and the United States. As a result, he was arrested and tried for treason at the end of the war, and spent the next 12 years in St Elizabeth's Hospital classified as a mental patient (he was diagnosed as having a narcissistic personality). He was released in 1958.

Pound returned to Rapallo with a young teacher he had met in hospital, Marcella Spann. He saw her as his last chance for love and a defence against old age. However, Dorothy managed to get her sent back to America.

In 1959 Pound began to suffer from depression, and began to doubt the value of his life's work. In his last published Canto (CXVI), he described his poetry as "a tangle of works unfinished". He was unable to finish *The Cantos*, though in 1969 he published *Drafts and Fragments of*

Cantos CX–CXVII.

He died in 1972, aged 87. Two weeks before he died, he repudiated his anti-Semitic rants against usury at a gathering of friends by reading a poem which included the words: "I was out of focus, taking a symptom for a cause. The cause is AVARICE."

* publications represented in the OIB syllabus selection are printed in bold.

PORTRAIT D'UNE FEMME

Your mind and you are our Sargasso Sea,
   London has swept about you this score years
And bright ships left you this or that in fee:
   Ideas, old gossip, oddments of all things,
Strange spars of knowledge and dimmed wares of price.   5
   Great minds have sought you — lacking someone else.
You have been second always. Tragical?
   No. You preferred it to the usual thing:
One dull man, dulling and uxorious,
   One average mind – with one thought less, each year. 10
Oh, you are patient, I have seen you sit
   Hours, where something might have floated up.
And now you pay one.   Yes, you richly pay.
   You are a person of some interest, one comes to you
And takes strange gain away: 15
   Trophies fished up; some curious suggestion;
Fact that leads nowhere; and a tale for two,
   Pregnant with mandrakes, or with something else
That might prove useful and yet never proves,
   That never fits a corner or shows use,   20
Or finds its hour upon the loom of days:
   The tarnished, gaudy, wonderful old work;
Idols and ambergris and rare inlays,
   These are your riches, your great store; and yet
For all this sea-hoard of deciduous things,   25
   Strange woods half sodden, and new brighter stuff:
In the slow float of differing light and deep,
   No! there is nothing! In the whole and all,
Nothing that's quite your own.
                Yet this is you.   30

- **Sargasso Sea** an area in the so-called Bermuda Triangle with extended mats of sargassum sea weed. Sea currents cause a great deal of miscellaneous debris to accumulate among the weeds.
- **Score**: an old word for the number 20.
- **uxorious**: excessively fond of or submissive to a wife.
- **mandrake**: a herb with a large forked root resembling a human in form and formerly credited with magical properties.
- **ambergris**: a waxy substance found floating in or on the shores of tropical waters, believed to originate in the intestines of the sperm whale, and used in perfumery as a fixative.

QUESTIONS

1. Where does the woman live?
2. What kind of social life does she lead?
3. What kinds of people seek her company?
4. What is the evidence that she is not married?
5. What is her opinion of the typical husband?
6. The contents of her mind are compared to a 'sea-hoard' – what strange objects are referred to as part of this hoard?
7. What point is Pound making about the contents of her mind?
8. Comment on the irony in line 24.
9. Re-read the last three lines. Is Pound's overall evaluation of this woman positive or negative? Why?
10. Read the definition of Sargasso Sea and explain how it is used as a metaphor to describe the woman and her mind? How is the metaphor extended in the next four lines?

11. How is the metaphor developed in the rest of the poem? Look particularly at lines 25 and 26.
12. Explain the meaning of line 6 (line 7 will give you a clue).
13. The poem is written as a direct address to the woman. How do you think she might respond? Re-read Pound's biography and make a list of things she might criticise in response.
14. One of Pound's aims when writing poetry at the time this was written (see Commentary) was "To use absolutely no word that does not contribute to the presentation." In your opinion, has he achieved this?
15. Another of his principles was: "As regarding rhythm: to compose in sequence of the musical phrase, not in sequence of the metronome." Count the syllables and stresses in the first five lines and analyse the verse form. When you have done this, comment on how far he has achieved his principle about rhythm.

COMMENTARY

This poem is from *Ripostes*, a collection of 25 poems published in London in February 1912. This is the first collection in which Pound puts into practice the ideas of the Imagist movement. A description of the Imagist movement's aims can be found on page 104.

Portrait d'une Femme is based on an extended image which is introduced in the first line – the Sargasso Sea (see note). She has collected "Ideas, old gossip, oddments of all things" from her conversations with "great minds" who have visited her only because they were unable to find any body else who to talk to. She has always been a "second" choice, but this is not "tragical" because she prefers it to living a conventional married life with one "dull" man with an "average" mind.

The poem continues with an extension of the Sargasso Sea metaphor: her mind is full of "trophies fished up" – in other words, the kinds of things that the currents might bring to the seaweed mats of the Sargasso sea: "mandrakes", "idols", "ambergris", "rare inlays". The phrase "sea-hoard" continues the metaphor still further, the word, "deciduous" suggesting that these things have been randomly shed from ships, like leaves from a deciduous tree: "strange woods half sodden, and new brighter stuff". The phrase "slow float" completes the metaphor. These lost objects float slowly in the Sargasso Sea. In literal terms, this is a vivid way of saying that her mind is full of miscellaneous odds and ends of information that she has picked up from her guests, many of whom are "great minds". The poem ends with harsh criticism, saying that all this is second-hand knowledge arising from other people's expertise, and that she has no specialist knowledge of her own.

We can see from the words "your" and "you" that this poem is a direct address to the "femme", woman, of the title. It is thus a rather unpleasant diatribe. It makes the reader wonder if the woman had offended Pound in some way. If so, there is no reference to it in the poem. Also, there is the arrogant assumption that the criticisms in the poem do not apply to the author; that he, in contrast, has a wide range of specialist knowledge that is all his own. The result of this is that the tone of the poem is satirical, mocking, patronising, though mitigated, perhaps, by a touch of ironic humour in the far-fetched nature of the central image.

How far does this poem fulfill Pound's Imagist

manifesto? To begin with, it is not written in free verse, but iambic pentameter, in other words, "the sequence of the metronome", and while the extended metaphor of the Sargasso Sea is striking, it is arguably laboured and verbose – it certainly does not make its impact "in an instant of time". On the whole, it has more in common with the metaphysical poetry of John Donne, who loved to develop elaborate geographical conceits, than with other Imagist poems.

UNE RIPOSTE D'UNE FEMME

The following poem is the author's attempt to answer the question about how the woman might respond. It is just a bit of fun, but worth reading because it contains some useful snippets of information about Pound's life.

Your mind and you are, as the critics said
when they reviewed your poetry in their journal,
"a medley of pretension"* – so much so,
you had to pay to have your first book published:
A Lume Spento, or "With Tapers Quenched"
translated into English.
I heard you nearly quenched the book yourself
by throwing all the proofs in the canal*.

So much for poetry – your private life
was even worse. I heard a dinner guest
was so annoyed with you he tried to stab you.
Your wife was ill – but did you succour her?
No, you took a mistress*, a young violinist,
Olga Rudge, and had a child by her*.
Now that's what I call "tragical!" – not me!

And now you dare to write a cruel satire

attacking one who never did you harm.
I do not have a "great mind" like my guests,
but from them I've learned much and they enjoy
my company – and in friendship is riches.

And what was written in Times Magazine*,
to characterise your personality? –
"a cat that walks by himself, tenaciously
unhousebroken and very unsafe for children."

Your poems are full of borrowings from others
and do not even rhyme. Your finest poem
is a translation from the Anglo-Saxon.
I've tried to find originality,
But there is nothing! In *Ripostes* and all;
nothing that's quite your own.
It's not dissimilar to what you say of me,
yet I am just a hostess – you pretend
to be a poet and thrust your mediocrity
onto the world and in your arrogance
and pretentiousness you call it genius.
Yet this is you –
I'd rather be me!

- *Canzoni* (1911) was criticised by *The Westminster Gazette* as a "medley of pretension".
- Pound wrote of *A Lume Spento* (1908), in Canto LXXVI: "should I chuck the lot into the tidewater?"
- In 1922 when he was 36 (she was 26).
- In 1933.
- Depending on when this imaginary 'riposte' was written, the 'femme' could have gone on to criticise his support for the Italian dictator,

Benito Mussolini, his many radio broadcasts supporting Fascism and his anti-Semitism, which led him to be arrested for treason after the war.

THE SEAFARER

The Seafarer is Pound's translation of a well-known Anglo-Saxon elegy dating from the 8th or 9th century. Our main focus is on Pound's unique approach to translation, rather than the poem itself, though a brief study of the original is a necessary starting point. For this reason, this chapter begins with a simplified translation of the original, and a short extract from the Anglo-Saxon text.

A SIMPLIFIED TRANSLATION

I can tell a true story about myself;
how I had to suffer bitter sorrows
and misfortunes while in a ship.
I was often drenched by high waves
while keeping night-watch at the prow.   5
My feet were pierced with cold
and frostbitten. I sighed with care,
suffered hunger pangs,
and the sea wolf's rage.
Those living happily on land   10
can never guess how miserable I was
on the ice-cold sea in winter,
an exile from my kin.

My ship was often hung with icicles,
the hail flew in stinging showers,   15
and I heard nothing
save the roaring of the sea.
Sometimes I heard a gannet's cry
and it reminded me of men's laughter,
or a seamew singing,   20
and that reminded me of mead-drinking,
but storms beat on the stony cliffs
where the starling, with icy wings,

13

and the eagle, screamed.
There was no hospitable kinsman   25
to shelter me. Those who enjoy life
on land, elated and wine-flushed
will never know how I,
tired and weary,
must endure night's darkening shadow,   30
snow from the north, frost and hail

It oppresses me to think
that I shall be tossed about like a toy
on the salt waves when I hope to find
a home, though among strangers.   35
But there is no man on earth
with such good qualities,
or such an ardent spirit
or such brave deeds,
or who was so favoured by his lord   40
that he does not fear how a future master
might treat him.

He does not enjoy the sound of the harp,
nor the receipt of rings,
nor delight in woman,   45
nor in any worldly joys,
but thinks of nothing else
but the rolling waves.

Flowery groves seem fair,
towns appear joyful,   50
the fields seem beautiful,
but the world hastens on
and one of three things will happen:
disease, or age, or the hostile sword
will destroy life.   55
So every man must work

14

against the hatred of foes,
by good deeds against the devil
so that, after him, the sons of men
may praise him, and his fame   60
live with angels for evermore
in the blessing of eternal life.

The good times are passed away;
all the pomps of earth's kingdom
are gone: there are no more gold-givers,   65
kings or emperors as of yore
when they lived in lordly power
and performed glories.
All this splendour is passed away,
and only weaker men remain.   70
Glory is humbled and the honours of the earth
have grown old and fade away.

Every man in Middle-Earth grows old,
his face grows pale, and his hair grey.
His friends are dead and buried,   75
and when he dies too, he will no longer
enjoy sweet things, nor move a hand, nor think,
and though his kindred fill his grave with treasure
he cannot take it with him.

*The following passage is probably a scribal addition, and is omitted in
Pound's translation:*

Gold cannot help a sinful soul,   80
or help a man who hides it
avoid God's wrath.
The fear of God is great,
for he created the earth and heaven above.
A man who does not fear God is foolish,   85
and comes to him unexpectedly.

Happy is he who lives humbly
for heaven's mercy comes to him.
A man should live with self-discipline and purity.
Every man should show moderation to both friend and foe.
Fate is hard, but the Creator is mightier
than any man's thought.
Let us consider where we have a home
and think how we might come there
and so prepare ourselves that we may go 95
into the eternal happiness
where life depends on the Lord's love.
Therefore let us give thanks
that the Chief of Glory, the Lord eternal
has honoured us. 100

The original poem is complex and confusing in places. The above translation (by the author) focuses on a clear presentation of the ideas in the poem, and makes no attempt to imitate the literary qualities. However, these can be analysed in the following short extract from the original text. Note that there is no correspondence of line numbers.

AN EXTRACT FROM THE ORIGINAL TEXT

The original text in *The Exeter Book* is set out in continuous lines, like prose, however, the usual convention for reprinting Anglo-Saxon poetry is to set it out in lines, consisting of two 'half-lines' separated by a space.

Mæg ic be me sylfum   soðgied wrecan,
siþas secgan,   hu ic geswincdagum
earfoðhwile   oft þrowade,
bitre breostceare gebiden hæbbe,
gecunnad in ceole   cearselda fela,   5
atol yþa gewealc,   þær mec oft bigeat

nearo nihtwaco   æt nacan stefnan,
þonne he be clifum cnossað   calde geþrungen
wæron mine fet,   forste gebunden
caldum clommum,   þær þa ceare seofedun   10
hat ymb heortan;   hungor innan slat
merewerges mod.   þæt se mon ne wat
þe him on foldan   fægrost limpeð,
hu ic earmcearig   iscealdne sæ
winter wunade   wræccan lastum,   15
winemægum bidroren,
bihongen hrimgicelum;   hægl scurum fleag.

THE SEAFARER, AS TRANSLATED BY EZRA POUND

May I for my own self song's truth reckon,
Journey's jargon, how I in harsh days
Hardship endured oft.
Bitter breast-cares have I abided,
Known on my keel many a care's hold,   5
And dire sea-surge, and there I oft spent
Narrow nightwatch nigh the ship's head
While she tossed close to cliffs. Coldly afflicted,
My feet were by frost benumbed.
Chill its chains are; chafing sighs   10
Hew my heart round and hunger begot
Mere-weary mood. Lest man know not
That he on dry land loveliest liveth,
List how I, care-wretched, on ice-cold sea,
Weathered the winter, wretched outcast   15
Deprived of my kinsmen;
Hung with hard ice-flakes, where hail-scur flew,
There I heard naught save the harsh sea
And ice-cold wave, at whiles the swan cries,
Did for my games the gannet's clamour,   20

Sea-fowls, loudness was for me laughter,
The mews' singing all my mead-drink.
Storms, on the stone-cliffs beaten, fell on the stern
In icy feathers; full oft the eagle screamed
With spray on his pinion.   25
Not any protector
May make merry man faring needy.
This he little believes, who aye in winsome life
Abides 'mid burghers some heavy business,
Wealthy and wine-flushed, how I weary oft   30
Must bide above brine.
Neareth nightshade, snoweth from north,
Frost froze the land, hail fell on earth then
Corn of the coldest. Nathless there knocketh now
The heart's thought that I on high streams   35
The salt-wavy tumult traverse alone.
Moaneth alway my mind's lust
That I fare forth, that I afar hence
Seek out a foreign fastness.
For this there's no mood-lofty man over earth's midst, 40
Not though he be given his good, but will have in his youth
greed;
Nor his deed to the daring, nor his king to the faithful
But shall have his sorrow for sea-fare
Whatever his lord will.
He hath not heart for harping, nor in ring-having   45
Nor winsomeness to wife, nor world's delight
Nor any whit else save the wave's slash,
Yet longing comes upon him to fare forth on the water.
Bosque taketh blossom, cometh beauty of berries,
Fields to fairness, land fares brisker,   50
All this admonisheth man eager of mood,
The heart turns to travel so that he then thinks
On flood-ways to be far departing.
Cuckoo calleth with gloomy crying,
He singeth summerward, bodeth sorrow,   55

The bitter heart's blood. Burgher knows not —
He the prosperous man — what some perform
Where wandering them widest draweth.
So that but now my heart burst from my breast-lock,
My mood 'mid the mere-flood,   60
Over the whale's acre, would wander wide.
On earth's shelter cometh oft to me,
Eager and ready, the crying lone-flyer,
Whets for the whale-path the heart irresistibly,
O'er tracks of ocean; seeing that anyhow   65
My lord deems to me this dead life
On loan and on land, I believe not
That any earth-weal eternal standeth
Save there be somewhat calamitous
That, ere a man's tide go, turn it to twain.   70
Disease or oldness or sword-hate
Beats out the breath from doom-gripped body.
And for this, every earl whatever, for those speaking after –
Laud of the living, boasteth some last word,
That he will work ere he pass onward,   75
Frame on the fair earth 'gainst foes his malice,
Daring ado,
So that all men shall honour him after
And his laud beyond them remain 'mid the English,
Aye, for ever, a lasting life's-blast,   80
Delight mid the doughty.
Days little durable,
And all arrogance of earthen riches,
There come now no kings nor Cæsars
Nor gold-giving lords like those gone.   85
Howe'er in mirth most magnified,
Whoe'er lived in life most lordliest,
Drear all this excellence, delights undurable!
Waneth the watch, but the world holdeth.
Tomb hideth trouble. The blade is layed low.   90
Earthly glory ageth and seareth.

No man at all going the earth's gait,
But age fares against him, his face paleth,
Grey-haired he groaneth, knows gone companions,
Lordly men are to earth o'ergiven,   95
Nor may he then the flesh-cover, whose life ceaseth,
Nor eat the sweet nor feel the sorry,
Nor stir hand nor think in mid heart,
And though he strew the grave with gold,
His born brothers, their buried bodies   100
Be an unlikely treasure hoard.

- **list**: listen
- **aye**: always
- **winsome**: attractive or appealing
- **bide**: wait
- **nathless**: nevertheless
- **fastness**: a secure place well protected by natural features
- **bosque**: forest
- **bodeth**: portends
- **laud**: praise
- **doughty**: brave and persistent.
- **seareth**: burns
- **gait**: manner of walking

QUESTIONS ON THE SIMPLIFIED TRANSLATION

1. What is the situation of the narrator of the The Seafarer?
2. Make a list of the things he has to suffer.
3. How does he see life on land? What else does he miss?
4. In line 13 the narrator describes himself as an

20

"exile". Find out about what it meant to be an exile in Anglo-Saxon times.

5. The narrator's suffering leads him to speculate on the fleeting qualities of life. Summarise these in your own words.

6. The last part of the poem was probably added by the monk who wrote down the poem (which had previously been passed on orally). How does it differ from the main part of the poem? Can you find any phrases in the main part of the poem which might also have been added by the monk?

QUESTIONS ON THE ORIGINAL TEXT

1. Anglo-Saxon poetry did not use rhyme, but was based on stress and alliteration. Each line is dived into two half-lines (indicated by a space), has four stressed syllables (underlined) and two or more stressed syllables which alliterate. Look at the first four lines to see how this is done, then try to annotate a few more lines yourself.

2. Compare the extract from the original with Pound's translation and see if you can identify any words and phrases. Make a short glossary. Here is a phrase to start you off: "nearo nihtwaco" – "narrow nightwatch".

QUESTIONS ON POUND'S TRANSLATION

1. Mark the alliteration and stressed syllables in the first 9 lines of Pound's translation. How far has he managed to reproduce the verse form of the original poem? Where has he varied from the pattern, and to what effect?

2. Anglo-Saxon is a very concrete language because many of the more abstract words were formed

from simple nouns, for example "breastcare" ("breostceare") is more concrete than "sorrow". Indeed, the word almost helps us to feel the sensation in our own body. In Pound's translation, find some similar examples, and comment on their effect when compared to the modern, abstract word.

3. Bearing in mind Pound's interest in Imagism, what do you think he found attractive in Anglo-Saxon poetry?

COMMENTARY

In early Anglo-Saxon times membership of a tribe was essential for security and well-being. There were no prisons in those days, so if you broke the law, or otherwise earned the disfavour of your lord, the only punishment was exile. As an exile, you would be deprived of companionship, in danger from enemies and robbers, and find it hard to procure the necessities of survival. *The Seafarer* is an elegy composed from the point of view of such an exile.

The exile begins with a vivid description of his sufferings in his ship in winter. He goes on to express regret for the loss of his home and kinsmen. From line 32 (note that line numbers do not correspond to the original text or Pound's translation) he expresses doubt that he will ever find a new lord who will treat him as well as he was treated before. From line 43 he uses the third person as he is speaking of humanity generally, and not just his own plight. His suffering has made him pessimistic about the plight of humanity, and he says that only three things can happen, "disease, or age, or the hostile sword" – all of them leading to death. The only remedy is to work against evil. The references to the "devil" and "angels" are almost certainly monkish interpolations, as the original was composed in the pre-Christian period. The exile goes on to lament the passing of the glorious and generous rulers he remembers. From line 73 he laments the losses of old age and the inevitability of death, with a final reflection on the worthlessness of treasure. Pounds translation ends at this point because what follows is almost certainly an addition by a monastic scribe. It is a series of commonplaces about trusting in God and preparing for heaven. The poem ends by giving thanks to God.

The extract from the original text gives an idea of the verse form used by Anglo-Saxon poets, and the concreteness of the Anglo-Saxon language, both of which Pound imitated in his translation. Pound focuses on these qualities rather than making an exact, scholarly translation, and in doing so preserves much of the sound and spirit of the original. His translation is difficult to read, so it is a good idea to focus on the first section and compare it with the Anglo-Saxon original.

In doing this, we find that Pound often preserves the Anglo-Saxon word order even when it sounds awkward in modern English. He tries to replicate the pattern of stress and alliteration in Anglo-Saxon verse form, lines 4 and 5 being "classic" examples (among many). However, he is not afraid to deviate from the form when necessary. For example, in line 6, he has placed the alliteration on the 4th stressed syllable (which is not allowed in Anglo-Saxon prosody). More strikingly, he writes several short lines, such as line 3.

He has used concrete Anglo-Saxon words rather than their abstract modern equivalents whereever he could do so without obscuring the meaning, for example:

- **bitter breastcares**: bitter sorrows
- **narrow nightwatch**: the claustrophic feeling of keeping watch at night
- **mere-weary**: weary of the sea
- **care-wretched**: made miserable by sorrow
- **scur**: no modern equivalent, but we sense the meaning of the word "scur" (it is related to modern English "scour".

This translation, though poetic rather than scholarly, is nevertheless greatly admired by scholars of Anglo-Saxon literature, one of whom, Michael Alexander, dedicated a book of scholarly translations to Pound (*The Earliest English Poems*, Michael Alexander, 1966).

If we look back at the aims of the Imagist movement (see page 104) we can see why this poem, along with other old poetry from many nations (including the Japanese Haiku) made a big impression on him. It showed that great poetry does not have to follow the conventions of rhyme and rhythm that had been used in English poetry since Chaucer, and that poetic language can be concrete rather than abstract.

THE GARDEN

En robe de parade.
　—SAMAIN

Like a skein of loose silk blown against a wall
She walks by the railing of a path in Kensington Gardens,
And she is dying piece-meal
of a sort of emotional anæmia.

And round about there is a rabble　　　　　　　　5
Of the filthy, sturdy, unkillable infants of the very poor.
They shall inherit the earth.

In her is the end of breeding.
Her boredom is exquisite and excessive.
She would like someone to speak to her,　　　　　10
And is almost afraid that I
will commit that indiscretion.

- The epigraph is from *Au Jardin de l'Infante,* which is the title of a collection of poems (1911) by Albert Samain. It means "dressed for show".
- **skein**: a length of loosely coiled thread
- **anæmia**: condition characterised by decreased red cells or haemoglobin in the blood causing tiredness, pallor, palpitations, shortness of breath.
- See *Matthew 5.5*: "Blessed are the meek, for they shall inherit the earth."

QUESTIONS

1. What clues are given about the social class of the woman?
2. What contrasts are there between her and the

children?

3. The phrase "emotional anæmia" is metaphorical. Read the definition of anæmia in the glossary, then try to explain what he means.

4. How does the last stanza add to our understanding of the woman's psychological condition?

5. What is the effect of the Biblical reference at the end of stanza 2?

6. What does the word "unkillable" suggest about Pound's attitude to these children?

7. What psychological conflict is presented in the last stanza? Suggest why she would like someone to speak to her, and why she would be afraid of the narrator (possibly Pound himself) doing so?

8. Consider the image in the first line in the light of what Pound said about the influence of the Japanese haiku on his poetry (see pp. 43-45ff.)

9. In what other ways does this poem fulfill the tenets of Imagism (see pages 43-45)?

10. Comment on the verse form of the poem if you have not already done so.

COMMENTARY

The poem is about an upper-middle class woman walking in Kensington Gardens (a royal park in an upmarket area of London). She is "dressed for show", presumably in one of the fashionable walking dresses of the time. She is contrasted with a group of poor children. She is suffering some kind of emotional fatigue, while they are "sturdy". Pound's use of the words "rabble", "filthy", and "unkillable" suggests that he dislikes them as much as she probably does, but he recognises their vigour, and believes that, as a result, they will, in the Biblical phrase, "inherit the earth", while the delicate and troubled middle classes will suffer "the end of breeding". He was wrong about that, of course, because the gap between rich and poor is still wide. The hardest thing to interpret is the woman's psychological state. She is not physically ill, but the seriousness of her condition is communicated in the phrase "dying piece-meal". Her condition is described by Pound as emotional anæmia. This, of course is a metaphor, and probably means that she is seriously lacking in emotional energy. This causes her to feel extremely bored. She desires social contact, but is too hidebound by social conventions to take advantage of opportunities to make friends. Thus, in the last few lines, Pound observes she seems afraid that he will speak to her. To understand better how Pound regards the overly-conventional middle classes, we need to relate this poem to other in this collection (*Lustra*). For example, *Salutation*, *Salutation the Second*, and *Commission*.

In this poem, Pound has achieved full expression of his Imagist manifesto (see page 104). The poem opens with a striking image, fulfilling his dictum that a good image is "that which presents an intellectual and emotional complex in an instant of time." It also shows the influence of the Japanese Haiku on his poetry (see pages 43-45). The poem is written with great economy, there being no superfluous verbiage (such as we see, perhaps, in *Portrait d'une Femme*), and is written in free verse. Free verse has no regular rhythm or rhyme, but gets its effect from line breaks – the first and last word of each line receiving a slight emphasis by the break. Each line has its own rhythm, which is the rhythm of natural language.

The tone of the poem is pitying. The point of view being that of a passive observer. At least he doesn't tell the woman what he thinks of her, as he does in *Portrait d'une Femme*. However, this is not personal. We will see in several other poems that Pound has a dislike for attitudes of the middle classes.

SALUTATION

O generation of the thoroughly smug
and thoroughly uncomfortable,
I have seen fishermen picnicking in the sun,
I have seen them with untidy families,
I have seen their smiles full of teeth   5
and heard ungainly laughter.

And I am happier than you are,
And they were happier than I am;
And the fish swim in the lake
and do not even own clothing.

- **smug**: too pleased or self-satisfied about something one has achieved.

QUESTIONS

1. To whom do you think is this poem addressed?
2. Who do you think is the speaker in the poem?
3. What hierarchy of happiness does the speaker present (who is the most happy, the next happy and the least happy?)
4. How does the comment about the fish tell us that the poem is, in part, a criticism of material possessions?
5. How does this poem meet Pounds criteria for Imagist poetry (see page 104)?

COMMENTARY

The poem is addressed to a "generation" – presumably Pound's contemporaries, young people in the middle and upper middle classes. They are "thoroughly smug" because they have benefitted from good education at private school and OXBRIDGE, have good professional jobs (or are gentlemen and women of leisure) and have large houses and many other material possessions. However, he believes that they are "thoroughly uncomfortable". He does not say why, but we can get some idea from the other poems in this collection (for example, the "emotional anæmia" of the woman in *The Garden*). He contrasts them to "fishermen picnicking in the sun", their happiness is evident from their smiles and their laughter (even if it is "ungainly").

He goes on to say that he is happier than the smug middle classes, though not as happy as the fisherman. The last two lines describe fish in the lake. There is no phrase of comparison, but the juxtaposition suggests that they are happiest of all, even though they own nothing, not even clothing. This suggests that the whole poem is a criticism of materialism. Those who have the most possessions are the least happy.

It could be argued that the poem is self-contradictory, because the narrator's attitude can also be described as "smug". He is, in effect, congratulating himself on not being like they are. Furthermore, his understanding of the fishermen is limited. A fisherman's life is hard and dangerous, so when they are unable to take a rare holiday, their enjoyment will proportionally much greater than those who lead lives of leisure. As for the fish, it's probably a struggle for survival down there!

The poem meets Pound's Imagist criteria in that it is written in free verse and with economy of expression. However, it does not contain any imagery, though the reference to the fish at the end of a poem is a kind of image as it makes the point about materialism in an a visual way.

SALUTATION THE SECOND

You were praised, my books,
because I had just come from the country;

I was twenty years behind the times
so you found an audience ready.

I do not disown you,   5
do not you disown your progeny.

Here they stand without quaint devices,
Here they are with nothing archaic about them.

Watch the reporters spit,
Watch the anger of the professors,   10
Watch how the pretty ladies revile them:

"Is this," they say, "the nonsense
that we expect of poets?"

"Where is the Picturesque?"
"Where is the vertigo of emotion?"   15

"No! his first work was the best."
"Poor Dear! he has lost his illusions."

Go, little naked and impudent songs,
Go with a light foot!
(Or with two light feet, if it please you!)   20
Go and dance shamelessly!
Go with an impertinent frolic!

Greet the grave and the stodgy,
Salute them with your thumbs at your noses.

30

Here are your bells and confetti.   25
Go! rejuvenate things!
Rejuvenate even "The Spectator."
Go! and make cat calls!
Dance and make people blush,
Dance the dance of the phallus   30
and tell anecdotes of Cybele!
Speak of the indecorous conduct of the Gods!
(Tell it to Mr. Strachey.)

Ruffle the skirts of prudes,
speak of their knees and ankles.   35
But, above all, go to practical people—
go! jangle their door-bells!
Say that you do no work
and that you will live forever.

- **progeny**: the offspring of.
- **quaint**: charmingly odd in an old-fashioned way.
- **archaic**: marked by the characteristics of an earlier period.
- **revile**: to speak abusively of.
- **Picturesque**: Picturesque is an aesthetic ideal introduced into English cultural debate in 1782 by William Gilpin; it refers to a kind of rugged beauty.
- **Vertigo**: a dizzying sensation.
- **The Spectator**: in 1909, this magazine praised Pound's work, saying he had "the capacity for remarkable poetic achievement."
- **cat-call**: a shrill whistle or shout of disapproval made at a public meeting or performance.
- **Cybele**: an Ancient Greek nature goddess worshipped with orgiastic rites.
- **Mr Strachey**: a literary friend who wrote a book entitled *Eminent Victorians* which Pound praised.

QUESTIONS

1. Pound gives two reasons why his early work was praised. What are they?
2. The third stanza implies that his style has changed, and the fourth describes that style. Rephrase his description in simple terms.
3. How does the public react to his new style?
4. What are they looking for in poetry? (lines 14 – 15). What does this show about their view of poetry?
5. Compare and contrast Pound's description description of his new poetry (lines 18ff) with the kind of people who will be shocked by them (lines 23ff).
6. What effect does he want them to have? What effect does he want them to have one "prudes" and "practical people"?
7. Which line shows that Pound has great confidence in the quality of his poems?
8. Describe the verse form of the poem, and examine the effect of some of the line breaks.
9. Comment on Pound's use of personification when describing how his poems will go out into the world (see lines 18-end).
10. The tone of the poem is humorous. Explain how this humorous tone is created.

COMMENTARY

In this poem, Pound reflects in a humorous way on his poetry and the effect it has one the public. He begins by saying that his early work was well received because it was "behind the times." Here are some samples of contemporary newspaper reviews:

Pound "is that rare thing among modern poets, a scholar...he has the capacity for remarkable poetic achievement" wrote a reviewer in the December, 1909 edition of *The Spectator*, about his first book, *A Lume Spento*.

The *Evening Standard*, commenting on the same book, said that it was "wild and haunting stuff, absolutely poetic, original, imaginative, passionate, and spiritual. Those who do not consider it crazy may well consider it inspired. Coming after the trite and decorous verse of most of our decorous poets, this poet seems like a minstrel of Provençe at a suburban musical evening.... The unseizable magic of poetry is in the queer paper volume, and words are no good in describing it."

However, *Canzoni* (1911) was criticised by the *Westminster Gazette* as a "medley of pretension".

The public, and many reviewers, believed that the mainstream style, referred to as "Georgian Poetry" (see pp. 123ff.) was what poetry should be like, hence the surprised questions:

Where is the Picturesque?
Where is the vertigo of emotion?

As can be seen in the note above, the "Picturesque" was a very outdated concept of beauty, and the idea that poetry should be emotional was very Victorian, founded on the work of poets such as Browning and Tennyson.

Lines 18 to the end contain a humorous personification of his poetry. He describes them as naked dancers who dance and frolic impertinently and shamelessly. He urges them to shock the public, especially the "grave and stodgy" – the same people who are described as "thoroughly smug" in *Salutation* – with cat calls and erotic dances and anecdotes. The poem ends by poking fun at "practical people". His poems are told to shock them by saying that they do no work but will live forever. (No wonder the general reading public preferred Georgian poetry to the insults of this bohemian modernist!)

The poem is written in free verse with many short stanzas. There is a great deal of anaphora (repetition) which provides a pattern to the poem, and emphasises key statements. Look, for example, at the lines beginning with "watch" or "where" or "go". Line breaks often emphasise key words, particularly at the end of lines. For example, a list of final words, would almost give an outline of the message in the poem.

The narrative perspective of the poem is the poet addressing his books – an odd idea which, from the first line, sets the humorous tone. The tone of humour is further developed by his delighted description of the shocked reaction of members of the public as varied as "professors" and "pretty ladies", and also by his striking personification of his dancing and impudent "songs".

COMMISSION

Go, my songs, to the lonely and the unsatisfied,
Go also to the nerve-racked, go to the
enslaved-by-convention,
Bear to them my contempt for their oppressors.
Go as a great wave of cool water,
Bear my contempt of oppressors.   5

Speak against unconscious oppression,
Speak against the tyranny of the unimaginative,
Speak against bonds.
Go to the bourgeoise who is dying of her ennuis,
Go to the women in suburbs.   10
Go to the hideously wedded,
Go to them whose failure is concealed,
Go to the unluckily mated,
Go to the bought wife,
Go to the woman entailed.   15

Go to those who have delicate lust,
Go to those whose delicate desires are thwarted,
Go like a blight upon the dullness of the world;
Go with your edge against this,
Strengthen the subtle cords,   20
Bring confidence upon the algae and the tentacles
of the soul.
Go in a friendly manner,
Go with an open speech.
Be eager to find new evils and new good,
Be against all forms of oppression.   25
Go to those who are thickened with middle age,
To those who have lost their interest.

Go to the adolescent who are smothered in family –

Oh how hideous it is
To see three generations of one house gathered together!
It is like an old tree with shoots,
And with some branches rotted and falling.

Go out and defy opinion,
Go against this vegetable bondage of the blood.
Be against all sorts of mortmain.   35

- **commission**: an instruction, command, or role given to a person.
- **bourgeois**: belonging to the middle class, with reference to its materialistic values and conventional attitudes.
- **ennui**: a feeling of utter weariness and discontent resulting from satiety or lack of interest; boredom. Note that Pound uses the plural form.
- **entailed**: legal term which in this context probably means "owned".
- **mortmain**: "dead hand", an expression which means the oppressive influence of past events.

QUESTIONS

1. Write a paragraph in which you describe the intended audience for Pound's poems. What kind of people are they, and what are their problems?
2. Which of these problems are of their own making?
3. How does Pound think his poems might help them?
4. Explain the following words and phrases: "enslaved-by-convention", "unconscious oppression", "hideously wedded", "failure is concealed", "all sorts of mortmain".
5. There are several powerful images in the poem.

Identify them, state what figure of speech is used, and explain their effect.

6. Comment on the effect of anaphora (repetition) in the poem.

7. Comment on the verse form of the poem and the effect of the line breaks.

8. How would you describe the tone of the poem?

9. What is the narrative stance of the poem?

10. How far does this poem suggest that Pound sees a social purpose in his poetry?

COMMENTARY

Pound is instructing his "songs" to go the kind of middle-class people whom he has targeted in several other poems. These are the middle classes who live in "suburbs" and are "enslaved by convention". They are victims of "all forms of oppression" (by this he means social conventions: marriage, family, job/career, etc.). He identifies some types specifically: there is a woman who is dying of boredom like the one in *The Garden*, there are the middle aged, and adolescents. He is particularly critical of the extended family, and the stultifying influence of the older generation. In the last three lines of his poem he expresses the hope that his poems will challenge them and the conventions that oppress them.

The poem is very different to the mainstream of Georgian poetry (see pp. 123ff.). The narrative stance (a poet speaking to his own poems) is unusual. The poem is written in free verse, but with strong natural rhythms, and line breaks that emphasise key words.

The tone of the poem is solemn and serious, and the mood imperative. This, and the anaphora on "go..."

reminds us of *Mark 16:15*, where Jesus says to his disciples: "Go into all the world and preach the Good News to everyone." It is clear that Pound believes that his poetry will have a similar, "saving" effect (though many might disagree with him!)

The starkness of the message, and the simplicity of the language is balanced by a series of vivid images which are good examples of his Imagist principles (see page 104).

The first (in line 4) is a simple simile, but its basis in nature gives it a similar effect to the Japanese haiku that Pound admired Perhaps the most vivid image in the poem (and the most Japanese) is in line 21: "Bring confidence upon the algae and the tentacles of the soul." Algae grows in stagnant water, and it therefore suggests a soul that is stagnant (showing no activity; dull and sluggish). "Tentacles" suggests the groping tentacles of an octopus which will eventually grasp and kill – in this case, it is the soul which will be killed. The image is powerful because of its complete contrast to the rest of the poem. Perhaps Pound is guilty of mixing his metaphors, and if he had been true to his Imagist aims he might have sacrificed the algae or the tentacles in the interests of economy.

The penultimate stanza contains a vivid image to describe the extended family:

It is like an old tree with shoots,
And with some branches rotted and falling

This is different from the algae/tentacles image because it provides an apt comparison to the subject and does not rely on the element of surprise. It is nevertheless, very powerful, though I have to say I do not agree with him as I believe that we have a duty to care for the elderly. However, "duty" is a word which Pound would perhaps consider to be one of those "forms of oppression" he is attacking.

Line 34 is also a mixed metaphor. Pound seems to be making a point in two very different ways. The word "vegetable" suggests "vegetating" (to live or spend a period of time in a dull, inactive, unchallenging way). "Bondage" (the state of being a slave) reinforces the ideas expressed in lines 8 and 25. What "blood" has got to do with it, I don't know. The Imagist tenet of economy would suggest that he should get rid of one of the metaphors – but perhaps Pound is developing his own special kind of "verbiage", very different from that of the Georgian poets, whom he was reacting against, but "verbiage" nonetheless.

In this poem, as in many others, Pound makes effective use of diction. "Ennuis" is interesting. The word is a borrowing from French, but is accepted (in its singular form, at least) as an English word. If you read the definition given in the glossary above, you will see why Pound chose it, as it has more force than the word "boredom". Also, it suggests a particular kind of middle-class boredom because only a middle class woman would think of her boredom using this sophisticated word.

THE BATH TUB

As a bathtub lined with white porcelain,
When the hot water gives out or goes tepid,
So is the slow cooling of our chivalrous passion,
O my much praised but-not-altogether-satisfactory lady.

QUESTIONS

1. What is the message in this poem?
2. What does the description of the bath convey about the social status of the woman.
3. Explain the image used to convey the message.
4. What does the word "chivalrous" suggest about their relationship?
5. Would it be chivalrous to say such a thing to a lady directly – or is it more likely that the poem represents what Pound was thinking?
6. The third line contains a conventional metaphor. What is it, and how does it relate to the main image?
7. Hyphens are used to join words (usually only two, when they represent one idea, for example: "check-in", "runner-up", "two-faced"). What idea does the long compound in the last line convey?
8. How far does this poem conform to Imagist principles (see page 104)?
9. Is it possible to detect the influence of Japanese poetry? (see page 127).

COMMENTARY

This short poem is a good example of Pound's Imagist principles and also the influence of Japanese poetry. It uses a single vivid image to describe the decline of passion in a relationship.

The description of the bath (called 'bathtub' by our American friends) suggests that the woman is one of the middle class women he often writes about. It is an expensive bath lined with porcelain. The words "chivalrous" and "lady" reinforce this idea. The central image (in the form of a simile) compares the cooling of the bathwater to the waning of their passion. The link between the two ideas is made stronger by the conventional metaphor "cooling" passion (conventional, because the word "cooling" is often used to describe fading emotions) and the literal description of the bathwater as "tepid". This word is often used in a metaphorical sense to describe feelings.

The word "chivalrous" suggests that they have behaved courteously and honourably to each other throughout their relationship so far, but Pound has realised that it will have to end. In view of this, it is unlikely that Pound is actually saying this to his lady. He is probably thinking it, and wondering what to do next.

The long compound word at the end of the poem suggests the reason for the cooling of his passion: that she fails to satisfy him in some way, though nothing specific is mentioned. This contrasts with the phrase "much praised" which suggests that he, has found many good reasons to praise her in the past, perhaps in his poetry. These two phrases can be seen as mapping the trajectory of the decline of passion.

The poem is Imagist in the sense that it uses free verse, is economical with words, and relies on a vivid image. It is also unconventional in that it is very different from the conventional love poems written by the Georgian poets (see an example on page 126).

IN A STATION OF THE METRO

The apparition of these faces in the crowd;
Petals on a wet, black bough.

QUESTIONS

1. Rewrite the poem in one simple English sentence linking the two ideas with the phrase "are like". Simplify the first line.
2. This poem was written under the direct influence of Japanese Haiku. Read about the haiku on pp. 127ff. and discuss the similarities and differences.
3. Parataxis is a literary technique in which two images are juxtaposed leaver the reader to work out the connection. Explain how parataxis is used in this poem.
4. In what sense is this a good example of Imagist principles? (see page 104).

COMMENTARY

I will leave it to Pound himself to explain this poem in words from *Gaudier-Brzeska*, 1916. More examples of haiku can be found on pp. 127ff.

Three years ago in Paris I got out of a "metro" train at La Concorde, and saw suddenly a beautiful face, and then another and another, and then a beautiful child's face, and then another beautiful woman, and I tried all that day to find words for what this had meant to me, and I could not find any words that seemed to me worthy, or as lovely as that sudden emotion. And that evening, as I went home along the Rue Raynouard, I was still trying and I found, suddenly, the expression. I do not mean that I found words, but there came an equation . . . not in speech, but in little splotches of colour. It was just that - a *"pattern,"* or *hardly a pattern, if by "pattern" you mean something with a "repeat" in it. But it was a word, the beginning, for me, of a language in colour... The Japanese have had the sense of exploration. They have understood the beauty of this sort of knowing. A Chinaman said long ago that if a man can't say what he has to say in twelve lines he had better keep quiet. The Japanese have evolved the still shorter form of the hokku.*

"The fallen blossom flies back to its branch:
A butterfly."

That is the substance of a very well-known hokku. Victor Plarr tells me that once, when he was walking over snow with a Japanese naval officer, they came to a place where a cat had crossed the path, and the officer said," Stop, I am making a poem." Which poem was, roughly, as follows: --

"The footsteps of the cat upon the snow:
(are like) plum-blossoms."

The words "are like" would not occur in the original, but I add them for clarity. The "one image poem" is a form of super-position, that is to say, it is one idea set on top of another. I found it useful in getting out of the impasse in which I had been left by my metro emotion. I wrote a thirty-line poem, and destroyed it because it was what we call work "of second intensity." Six months later I made a poem half that length; a year later I made the following hokku-like sentence: --

"The apparition of these faces in the crowd:
Petals, on a wet, black bough."

I dare say it is meaningless unless one has drifted into a certain vein of thought. I a poem of this sort one is trying to record the precise instant when a thing outward and objective transforms itself, or darts into a thing inward and subjective.

WRITE YOUR OWN POUND/METRO POEM
(with the help of five famous Japanese poets)

Begin with a long title, e.g., "On a Bus Going to Serangoon".

Write the first line in the present tense. Something trivial and everyday works well. For best effect, use a pentameter, like Pound, e.g:

People with blank faces sit and stare

Then roll a dice to give you the second line from this list taken from famous Japanese poets:

1. a frog jumps into the pond (Matsuo Basho)
2. the clouds give rest to the moon-beholders (Matsuo Basho)
3. leaves gather in the east (Yosa Buson)
4. winds howl in rage with no leaves to blow (Natsume Soseki)
5. a hawk descending on a day in spring (Masaoka Shiki)
6. the mirror I stare into shows my father's face (Murakami Kijo)

Here is an example:

ON A BUS GOING TO SCHOOL

People with blank faces sit and stare;
a hawk descending on a day in spring.

45

WALKING TO SCHOOL ON A MONDAY MORNING

I check my mobile phone for messages;
winds howl in rage with no leaves to blow.

AFTER SCHOOL

It's been a hard day;
the mirror I stare into shows my father's face.

Feel free to experiment, as in this example:

IN THE BUS STATION IN ANG MO KIO

They wait
dulled by the prospect of another working day;
leaves gather in the east.

Read again the description of the Haiku form on pp. 127ff., and experiment freely with different numbers of syllables, line lengths, and different kinds of juxtaposition/parataxis.

THE RIVER-MERCHANT'S WIFE: A LETTER

While my hair was still cut straight across my forehead
I played about the front gate, pulling flowers.
You came by on bamboo stilts, playing horse;
You walked about my seat, playing with blue plums.
And we went on living in the village of Chokan: 5
Two small people, without dislike or suspicion.

At fourteen I married My Lord you.
I never laughed, being bashful.
Lowering my head, I looked at the wall.
Called to, a thousand times, I never looked back.   10

At fifteen I stopped scowling,
I desired my dust to be mingled with yours
Forever and forever, and forever.
Why should I climb the look-out?

At sixteen you departed,   15
You went into far Ku-to-Yen, by the river of
swirling eddies,
And you have been gone five months.
The monkeys make sorrowful noise overhead.
You dragged your feet when you went out.
By the gate now, the moss is grown, the different mosses,
Too deep to clear them away!
The leaves fall early this autumn, in wind.
The paired butterflies are already yellow with August
Over the grass in the west garden—
They hurt me.   25
I grow older.
If you are coming down through the narrows of the river,

Please let me know beforehand,
And I will come out to meet you,
  As far as Cho-fu-Sa.

From the Chinese of Li Po.

- Cho-fu-Sa is hundreds of miles way from Chokan.

QUESTIONS

1. This letter tells the story of a relationship. Read it carefully and retell the story in simple terms.
2. From a western point of view, what is surprising about stanza two?
3. What expression does she use to express her deep love for her husband in stanza three?
4. In stanza four, her sorrow is expressed indirectly – explain how, and comment on the effect.
5. What words tell us that her husband was reluctant to leave?
6. What image does she use at the end of this stanza to indicate the passing of time?
7. How else does she indicate the passing of time?
8. Why do the "paired butterflies" hurt her?
9. Read the note about Cho-fu-Sa, and say how this line shows her love.
10. Read about Pound's reaction to his discovery of Chinese poetry in the first paragraph of the commentary, then see if you can find any of the qualities he admires in this poem.
11. How does Chinese poetry (judging from this example) fit in with the aims of the Imagist movement? (see page 104).
12. Compare and contrast Pound's translation with the literal translation (extract) and the alternative translation in the commentary.

COMMENTARY

Pound was introduced to Chinese poetry in 1913 when Mary McNeil Fenollosa asked him to organise the papers of her late husband, Ernest Fenollosa, which included translations of Chinese Taoist poetry. Pound saw that the poetry was "terse, polished and emotionally suggestive", and produced his own versions of fifteen of the poems which were published in *Cathay* in 1915.

The poem is written in the form of a letter from a wife to her husband. It is organised by the girl's age. The first stanza is early childhood, the second when she is 14, the third when she is 15, and the fourth, the present time, when she is sixteen. Pound, like many other translators, chose to use free verse for his version of the poem, though the original Chinese poem is highly patterned and makes use of rhyme (see below for details)

She begins by reminiscing about their friendship in childhood, giving us a glimpse of their lives through a few vivid details. Her hair "cut straight" is clearly a style of haircut associated with children in 8th century China. "Bamboo stilts" and "playing with blue plums" are the games of young children. The first stanza ends with a comment on their childhood innocence.

The first line of the second stanza is striking, and not only because her early marriage is surprising (shocking to some) by western standards, and because of her subservient position in the relationship. The awkward word order suggests direct translation from the Chinese characters (though a closer analysis shows that this is not the case – see below). She recalls how very shy she was and emphasises it with a visual image of her lowering her head and looking at the wall even though she was called to a thousand times. This is even more powerfully expressed in the Chinese original (see commentary).

The third stanza expresses how deeply she has come to love her husband (even though their marriage would have been arranged). This is expressed in a powerful image of mingling dust, and repetition of "forever"

In the last stanza she alludes indirectly to her sorrow by her interpretation of the sounds made by the monkeys. The passing of time is shown by the vivid image of the mosses, and the falling of the autumn leaves.

The image of the "paired butterflies" is the most potent in the whole poem, especially when linked with the phrase "they hurt me". They are a reminder of the close companionship and love that she is missing. The images of the passing of time are rounded of with the phrase "I grow older". As in much Chinese and Japanese poetry, a few words are used to suggest a great deal. These three words express that she feels that her life is being wasted while she is living without her husband.

The last three lines, re-establish the letter form, and give a final, and powerful expression in love. She is prepared to walk a very long way in order to see her husband as soon as possible.

If we measure this poem against Pound's Imagist manifesto (see page 104) we see that every aspect of it is fulfilled. Pound must have been surprised and delighted to find that his ideas about poetry had been anticipated in Ancient China.

Like Pound's translation of the Seafarer, this poem, and the others in *Cathay*, are poetic, rather than scholarly translations, as can be seen by comparing the above poem to the original text and Arthur Waley's translation below.

THE ORIGINAL TEXT

On the next page you will find the original poem in Chinese characters. Note that there are five characters per line. Each character is an ideogram expressing an idea. The sounds of the last characters in the lines rhyme and the pattern is shown in the transliteration.

長干行　李白

妾髮初覆額　折花門前劇
郎騎竹馬來　遶牀弄青梅
同居長干里　兩小無嫌猜
十四為君婦　羞顏未嘗開
低頭向暗壁　千喚不一迴
十五始展眉　願同塵與灰
常存抱柱信　豈上望夫臺
十六君遠行　瞿塘灩澦堆
五月不可觸　猿聲天上哀
門前遲行跡　一一生綠苔
苔深不能掃　落葉秋風早
八月胡蝶黃　雙飛西園草
感此傷妾心　坐愁紅顏老
早晚下三巴　預將書報家
相迎不道遠　直至長風沙

Here is a transliteration of the characters in the first five lines (with letters showing the rhyme scheme).

CHANG GAN TRAVEL

concubine hair young cover forehead	a
collect flower gate in-front-of play	b
young-man ride bamboo horse come	c
around trellis play blue plums	c
together reside Chang Gan village	a
couple small have no hate conjecture	c
fourteen be sovereign wife	b
shy face not-yet experience initiate	c
hang head towards dark wall	a
thousand call not one turn-round	d

A much more detailed analysis of the original can be found here: http://www.textetc.com/workshop/wt-li-po-1.html

AN ALTERNATIVE TRANSLATION

This following translation is by Arthur Waley (1889 – 1966), who was an English Orientalist who achieved both popular and scholarly acclaim for his translations of Chinese and Japanese poetry.

CH'ANG-KAN

Soon after I wore my hair covering my forehead
I was plucking flowers and playing in front of the gate,
When you came by, walking on bamboo-stilts
Along the trellis, playing with the green plums.
We both lived in the village of Ch'ang-kan,   5
Two children, without hate or suspicion.

At fourteen I became your wife; I was shame-faced and
never dared smile.
I sank my head against the dark wall;
Called to a thousand times, I did not turn.   10
At fifteen I stopped wrinkling my brow
And desired my ashes to be mingled with your dust.
I thought you were like the man who clung to the bridge:
Not guessing I should climb the Look-for-Husband Terrace,
But next year you went far away,   15
To Ch'ü-t'ang and the Whirling Water Rocks.
In the fifth month "one should not venture there"
Where wailing monkeys cluster in the cliffs above.
In front of the door, the tracks you once made
One by one have been covered by green moss—   20
Moss so thick that I cannot sweep it away,
And leaves are falling in the early autumn wind.
Yellow with August the pairing butterflies
In the western garden flit from grass to grass.
The sight of these wounds my heart with pain;   25
As I sit and sorrow, my red cheeks fade.
Send me a letter and let me know in time
When your boat will be going through the three gorges of
Pa.
I will come to meet you as far as ever you please,
Even to the dangerous sands of Ch'ang-kan.   30

Li Po
Translation by Arthur Waley

LAMENT OF THE FRONTIER GUARD

By the North Gate, the wind blows full of sand,
Lonely from the beginning of time until now!
Trees fall, the grass goes yellow with autumn.
I climb the towers and towers
to watch out the barbarous land: 5
Desolate castle, the sky, the wide desert.
There is no wall left to this village.
Bones white with a thousand frosts,
High heaps, covered with trees and grass;
Who brought this to pass?   10
Who has brought the flaming imperial anger?
Who has brought the army with drums and with kettle-drums?
Barbarous kings.
A gracious spring, turned to blood-ravenous autumn,
A turmoil of wars − men, spread over the middle kingdom
Three hundred and sixty thousand,
And sorrow, sorrow like rain.
Sorrow to go, and sorrow, sorrow returning,
Desolate, desolate fields,
And no children of warfare upon them,   20
No longer the men for offence and defence.
Ah, how shall you know the dreary sorrow at the North Gate,
With Rihoku's name forgotten,
And we guardsmen fed to the tigers.

By Rihaku (Li Po)

QUESTIONS

1. This poem tells a story of war and suffering. Rewrite that story in simple terms.
2. How does the guard express his loneliness?
3. How is the passing of time indicated?
4. What images suggest the desolation of the village?
5. Comment on the adjectives used in line 14.
6. Explain the effect of the simile in line 17.
7. Comment on the use of repetition in lines 17 – 19.
8. What is your interpretation of the last line?
9. Compare Pound's version with the version by Arthur Roberts in the Commentary.

COMMENTARY

The poem is called a Lament and it begins with the border guard describing the uncomfortable conditions, his loneliness, and his sense of having been there for an interminable time. As he describes his surroundings, a story begins to unfold. The village walls have been destroyed and heaps of white bones are scattered around. This is the result of an attack by three hundred and sixty thousand of the Emperor's soldiers. The attack has devastated the village. The fields are 'desolate' (barren/laid waste), and no men remain of either side. The guard ends his lament by emphasising his sorrow. Rihoku, who presumably was lord of the region, is forgotten, and the guard is living in fear. The last line is open to interpretation, but it could mean that he feels he is vulnerable to an attack by a tiger, as he is now alone, and the village walls are broken, or more probably it is metaphorical, meaning that he, and guards like him, are neglected and left vulnerable to any danger.

It is interesting to compare Pound's version with Arthur Roberts'. Roberts chose to use traditional rhythm and rhyme in his translation, and it is clear that some accuracy of meaning has been sacrificed. However, the patterns of rhyme and rhythm are perhaps a better reflection of the patterns of the original, which has a set number of characters per line and also rhymes. Furthermore, there is a terseness and economy about the poem which is reinforced by the metre and rhyme. It has been said that Pound "invented" the English version of Chinese poetry, and he did it in his own style as an Imagist poet. But it can be seen from a close inspection of Chinese originals (see the analysis of the original of *The River-Merchant's Wife*) that Chinese poetry is something very different indeed from what either Pound, Waley or Roberts have made of it. To paraphrase what Bentley said of Pope's Iliad, "It is a pretty poem, Mr. Pound, but you must not call it Li Po." (Actually, he didn't, Pound attributed the poems in *Cathay* to a fictional Chinese poet whom he named Rihaku, but the point remains valid).

THE FRONTIER GUARD'S LAMENT

By the North Gate the wind blows sand.
It is a lonely place to stand,
and bleak when Autumn casts its pall,
and grass turns yellow and leaves fall.

I climb the battlements and towers   5
and watch the land for endless hours;
the desolate castle and the sky,
the village – though I don't know why:

the wall has tumbled to the ground,
whitened bones are strewn around,   10
heaps of them, covered with grass.
Who brought this tragedy to pass?

Who brought the village into danger?
Who brought the army here in anger?
Who brought the kettledrums and swords?   15
Who brought the Emperor's warlords?

Spring was green; Autumn blood-red;
turmoil of wars and thousands dead;
and sorrow, sorrow like the rain,
daily sorrow, daily pain.   20

Desolate fields rotting away,
no children now to sing and play,
or men to fight or to defend,
or struggle for who knows what end?

How shall you know the depth of sorrow?   25
At the North Gate there's no tomorrow:
Our Lord, Rihoku, is long dead;
And to the tigers we are fed.

Translation from Li Po by Arthur Roberts

p 74

THE CITY OF CHOAN

The phoenix are at play on their terrace.
The phoenix are gone, the river flows on alone.
Flowers and grass
Cover over the dark path
where lay the dynastic house of the Go.   5
The bright cloths and bright caps of Shin
Are now the base of old hills.
The Three Mountains fall through the far heaven,
The isle of White Heron
splits the two streams apart.   10
Now the high clouds cover the sun
And I can not see Choan afar
And I am sad.

Before reading the poem, read the first two paragraphs of the commentary which give important background information.

QUESTIONS

1. What is the effect of the contrast between "bright cloths" and "bright caps" and "the base of old hills"?

2. What does it suggest about the time that has elapsed since Choan was sacked and the time the poem was written?

3. The word "fall" in line 8 is unexpected. What does it suggest about how the poet sees the mountains?

4. In lines 11 and 12, the darkening sky prevents the poet from seeing the ruins of Choan. What might this symbolise?

5. Read the last line and explain why the poet is sad.

6. Compare this last line with the last line of Bynner's translation (see pp. 61) and say which you prefer and why.

7. Compare the rest of the two translations. Are there places where Bynner's version seems preferable – why?

COMMENTARY

The city of Choan is modern Quanzhou (泉州). It was the base of the Southern Chen dynasty, the fourth and last of the Southern Dynasties in China, eventually destroyed by the Sui dynasty by general Yang Su in the 590s. The city was re-established in 718, when Li Po was 18. This poem is a reflection on the desolation of the city of Choan many years after its conquest, and was, no doubt, inspired by teh rebuilding of the city.

The poem begins with an image of "phoenix at play". In Greek mythology, the phoenix is a symbol of rebirth, which would be highly appropriate for this poem. However, in Chinese mythology, the phoenix is a symbol of heaven's favour, luck and happiness. Significantly, the poet writes in the second line: "the phoenix are gone", telling us that heaven's favour, luck and happiness have departed from Choan. This tells us that the poet is imagining a time before the rebuilding of the city.

The adjective "dark" in line 4 perhaps hints at some of the dark deeds that took place during the battle. "Flowers and grass" suggest that time has covered this reminder of the past with natural beauty. Bynner's translation makes more sense at this point, showing that Li Po is indicating that both rival dynasties are long forgotten (see below).

The "two streams" in line 10 are the Jin and Luo rivers as they flow into Quanzhou Bay on the Taiwan Strait.

The poem ends with a vivid picture of the present moment (for the poet): the clouds have covered the sun and he cannot see Choan in the distance. This is symbolic of the destruction of Choan. The last line is an expression of sorrow which is powerful in its simplicity, and a good example of what Pound means by "economy of language", especially if we compare Bynner's version.

AN ALTERNATIVE TRANSLATION

The following translation is by Harold Witter Bynner (1881 – 1968), an American poet, writer and scholar.

ON CLIMBING IN NANKING TO THE TERRACE OF PHOENIXES

Phoenixes that played here once, so that the place was named for them,
Have abandoned it now to this desolate river;
The paths of Wu Palace are crooked with weeds;
The garments of Chin are ancient dust.
...Like the green horizon halving the Three Peaks,   5
Like this island of White Egrets dividing the river,
A cloud has arisen between the Light of Heaven and me,
To hide his city from my melancholy heart.

Witter Bynner and Kiang Kang-Hu

This is how Hugh Kenner compared the two translations in his book *The Poetry of Ezra Pound*, 1985.

It will be noticed that Mr. Bynner has, in the first line, inserted an explanatory detail; in the second, replaced the Chinese formal articulation (parallelism) with the English grammatical; in the fifth and sixth added the wholly unjustified "like this" for the sake of imaginary poetic articulation; and in the last couplet arbitrarily turned a semi-symbolic statement into a metaphoric. Mr Pound's version is at once good poetry and a faithful translation.

HUGH SELWYN MAUBERLEY

(PARTS IV AND V)

IV.

These fought, in any case,
and some believing, pro domo, in any case
Some quick to arm,
some for adventure,
some from fear of weakness,   5
some from fear of censure,
some for love of slaughter, in imagination,
learning later .
some in fear, learning love of slaughter;
Died some pro patria, non dulce non et decor . .   10
walked eye-deep in hell
believing in old men's lies, then unbelieving
came home, home to a lie,
home to many deceits,
home to old lies and new infamy ;   15
usury age-old and age-thick
and liars in public places.
Daring as never before, wastage as never before.
Young blood and high blood,
Fair cheeks, and fine bodies;   20
fortitude as never before
frankness as never before,
disillusions as never told in the old days,
hysterias, trench confessions,
laughter out of dead bellies.   25

V.

Here died a myriad,
And of the best, among them,
For an old bitch gone in the teeth,
For a botched civilization,
Charm, smiling at the good mouth,   5
Quick eyes gone under earth's lid,
For two gross of broken statues,
For a few thousand battered books.

- **pro domo**: for home.
- **pro patria**: for your native land.
- **non dulce non et decor**: an incomplete quotation which means: "it is not sweet and not fitting to die for your country". See the poem by Wilfred Owen on page 70.
- **usury**: lending money at unreasonably high rates of interest.
- **Gross**: an old word for the number 144.

QUESTIONS

1. Read lines 1 to 9, then state in your own words the reasons why men joined up to fight in the First World War. Give a short explanation for each reason.
2. Are any of these good reasons?
3. What does Pound believe to be the main reason?
4. Line's 10 – 12 make reference to a famous poem by Wilfred Owen which is reprinted on page 70. Read the extract, then explain what Pound is saying in line 10.
5. The repeated word "lie" in lines 12-15, also alludes

to Owen's poem, but as well as the "old lie" there are new lies and deceits – what are they?

6. Who is Pound thinking of when he mentions usury?

7. Who is he thinking of when he mentions "liars in public places?"

8. Speculate about what Pound might mean when he writes: "wastage as never before".

9. What do you think is meant by "high blood" in line 19?

10. Look up the meanings of the words "fortitude" and "frankness" and consider how war could have developed these qualities.

11. Lines 23 and 24 discuss the psychological problems that war causes. Explain each one in your own words.

12. What do you think Pound means by line 25?

13. In Part V, what do you think Pound means when he describes Western civilisation as "an old bitch gone in the teeth?"

14. Why does he call it "botched"?

15. Who is referred to in lines 5 and 6?

16. At the end of Part V, Pound sums up the achievement of western civilisation as "two gross of broken statues" and "a few thousand battered books". What does he mean? Is this a fair summation of western civilisation?

17. What is the verse-form of the poem?

18. Find places where a line break, or a short, or a long line has been used to emphasise meaning.

19. How is repetition/anaphora used in the poem?

20. Explain line 11. What figure of speech is used and what is its effect?

21. Explain the figure of speech in Part V, line 6, and comment on its effect.

22. What word or words would you use to describe the tone of the poem. Quote some words and phrases

from the poem that help to create this tone.

23. The critic, F. R. Leavis, described this poem as a "turning point" in Pound's poetic development. What is it about the style of this poem that differs from his earlier, Imagist, poetry?

24. Compare and contrast *Mauberley*, Parts IV and V, with *Dulce et Decorum Est*, and say which poem conveys the most powerful anti-war message and why.

COMMENTARY

This poem consists of 18 parts, and describes a poet whose life has become empty and meaningless. It begins with a satirical analysis of the London literary scene, and continues with social criticism, economics, and an attack on the causes of the war. The poem is regarded by some critics as Pound's major achievement. There is much debate about how far the character of Mauberley is autobiographical, though this issue does not affect stanzas IV and V, which are a direct protest against the war. Stanza V expressed Pound's disgust at the waste of life because he doesn't think western civilisation was worth dying for.

Mauberley was published in June 1920 and marked Pound's farewell to London. He had decided to leave England because he was unable to reconcile himself to the great loss of life during the war.

It begins with a discussion of the reasons young men joined up to fight, In the first two lines "in any case" is repeated in a way that seems almost clumsy, but it emphasises that whatever the variety of reasons almost all young men joined up.

It is interesting that in Pound's list of reasons, most are negative and three are to do with types of fear. Two of the reasons are explained using Latin quotations ("pro domo" ad "pro patria"). Latin was one of the most important subjects in private schools, and these well-known phrases were used to persuade young men to join up.

"Non dulce non et decor..." is an example of Pound's use of intertextual references – a technique that he used increasingly in his later poems, particularly *The Cantos*. It is an allusion to a famous quotation from an Ode of Horace, and to Wilfred Owen's poem on the saying (see below). Owen calls it "the old lie" ("old" because it has been used since the first century BC), and Pound picks up this idea when he writes about lies in lines 12 and 13. Also, "walked eye-deep in hell" is an abstract way of referring to the horrors that Owen describes in excruciating detail.

The "new infamy" that soldiers come home to is "usury". This is the first time that Pound has used this word, and it is the beginning of a concerted attack against Jewish bankers in his later work, and in his wartime broadcasts in support of Fascism. The "liars in public places" are probably politicians – not much changes: bankers (of all races!) have earned a bad reputation in recent years, and the Brexit referendum was notable for lies on both sides of the debate. From lines 18 to 25, Pound contrasts the very fine physical qualities and qualities of character of the young soldiers with the terrible psychological consequences: "disillusions", "hysterias", "confessions". Part V ends with a vivid image to reinforce this idea. It is hard to explain it literally, but its force is beyond doubt. The laughter is, of course, hysterical laughter, and the word "dead" perhaps means that the young men have been psychologically destroyed by war.

Part V is a bitter attack on western civilisation. Why does "civilisation" come into this? – Probably because WWI was often described as "The Great War for Civilisation" (These words were inscribed on the "Victory" medal awarded to all British servicemen and women). That was how many people felt at the time, though presumably, if the outcome of the war had been different, western civilisation would have carried on in much the same way.

Pound describes western civilisation with the powerful image of "an old bitch gone in the teeth". This contains a powerful insult and suggestion that western civilisation has lost its power. However, this is not a valid argument, but merely verbal abuse. Indeed, the whole of this part is nothing more than an emotional outburst to sway the readers' sentiments instead of their minds. He goes on to say that civilisation "botched", though does not give any supporting evidence. Of course, it is a poem, not an essay, but Owen does a much better job by arguing against war on the grounds of inhumane suffering supported by a very detailed example.

Pound then compares the beauty the young men (lines 5 and 6) with what they have died for, which he sums up as "two gross of broken statues" and "a few thousand battered books". These two things are a synecdoche (a figure of speech in which the part stands for the whole) for all the achievements of western civilisation. But the fact that he can sum up the achievement of western civilisation in such reductive terms show the depths of his disillusionment.

The tone of the poem is extremely bitter, scathing, acrimonious, even hate-filled. This tone is created by words such as: "lies", "deceits", "infamy", "disillusions", "hysterias" and phrases such as: "laughter out of dead bellies", "an old bitch gone in the teeth".

67

The verse form is free verse patterned by extensive use of repetition, which in some places reads with the incantatory effect of a chant, for example, lines 3 to 9. Key words and phrases are repeated for emphasis: "in any case", "fear", "slaughter", "lie/lies/liars", "domo/home". The repetition is reinforced by the list-like nature of some passages. Lines 3 to 9 are a list of reason why young men joined up, lines 13 – 17 are a list of what the young men faced when they came home, and their psychological sufferings are listed in lines 23 – 25. The listing goes on in Part V. Lines 5 and 6 list the wonderful qualities of human beings and the last two lines list two of the main things that characterise western civilisation. Pound's free verse lines usually consist of a unit of speech marked by natural speech rhythm, and the line breaks often emphasise a key word, for example, in lines 5 to 11, the reasons which prompted the young men to join up are often indicated at the end of the line.

The critic F. R. Leavis described this poem as a "turning point" in Pound's poetic development, and it is, indeed, very different from his Imagist poems. If we look back at his Imagist manifesto on page 104, we can see the changes. Pound is still writing free verse: "compose in sequence of the musical phrase, not in sequence of the metronome", but he is no longer attempting "direct treatment of the 'thing'". Instead, he is talking about the 'thing', and rather abstractly at that. It is interesting to compare Pound's anti-war rant (for that is how it comes across) to Owen's best-known war poem, *Dulce Et Decorum Est* (see page 70). Owen does not rant; he does not preach at us; he does not abuse bankers, politicians, or some abstract concept of western civilisation, he simply describes the suffering of a soldier caught in a gas attack in the most vivid and excruciating detail, and then poses the question, with reference to the often-used Latin quotation from Horace: "is it really sweet and fitting to die for your country"?

Pound is no longer using the kind of image "which presents an intellectual and emotional complex in an instant of time", or juxtaposing an image against a description as he did in *In A Station of the Metro* and his translations of Chinese poems. The images in these extracts from *Mauberley* are few and generalised. The only example of the juxtaposition of an image is "laughter out of dead bellies" but this is not the same kind of specific image as "petals on a wet, black bough", because it does not refer to a specific 'thing'; a specific belly, a specific soldier. By contrast, Owen's poems gives us a series of vivid images which help us to imagine the agonising death of a particular soldier:

> Dim through the misty panes and thick green light,
> As under a green sea, I saw him drowning.

Nevertheless, these two parts of Mauberley have a power of their own which is different from Pound's earlier Imagist work, or from Owen's stark realism. Throughout this extract, the young men are contrasted with the civilisation, and the people they died for, and the stark message is driven home by skilfully patterned free verse and cleverly juxtaposed ideas.

DULCE ET DECORUM EST

by Wilfred Owen.

Bent double, like old beggars under sacks,
Knock-kneed, coughing like hags, we cursed through sludge,

Till on the haunting flares we turned our backs,
And towards our distant rest began to trudge.
Men marched asleep. Many had lost their boots,   5
But limped on, blood-shod. All went lame; all blind;
Drunk with fatigue; deaf even to the hoots
Of gas-shells dropping softly behind.

Gas! GAS! Quick, boys!—An ecstasy of fumbling
Fitting the clumsy helmets just in time,   10
But someone still was yelling out and stumbling
And flound'ring like a man in fire or lime.—
Dim through the misty panes and thick green light,
As under a green sea, I saw him drowning.

In all my dreams before my helpless sight,   15
He plunges at me, guttering, choking, drowning.

If in some smothering dreams, you too could pace
Behind the wagon that we flung him in,
And watch the white eyes writhing in his face,
His hanging face, like a devil's sick of sin;   20
If you could hear, at every jolt, the blood
Come gargling from the froth-corrupted lungs,
Obscene as cancer, bitter as the cud
Of vile, incurable sores on innocent tongues,—
My friend, you would not tell with such high zest   25
To children ardent for some desperate glory,
The old Lie: Dulce et decorum est
Pro patria mori*.

- "It is sweet and fitting to die for your country". This famous quotation is from an ode by the Latin poet Horace (Quintus Horatius Flaccus (65 BC – 8 BC) which was written to encourage Roman citizens to fight against the Parthians.

CANTO I

And then went down to the ship,
Set keel to breakers, forth on the godly sea, and
We set up mast and sail on that swart ship,
Bore sheep aboard her, and our bodies also
Heavy with weeping, so winds from sternward   5
Bore us out onward with bellying canvas,
Circe's this craft, the trim-coifed goddess.
Then sat we amidships, wind jamming the tiller,
Thus with stretched sail, we went over sea till day's end.
Sun to his slumber, shadows o'er all the ocean,   10
Came we then to the bounds of deepest water,
To the Kimmerian lands, and peopled cities
Covered with close-webbed mist, unpierced ever
With glitter of sun-rays
Nor with stars stretched, nor looking back from heaven 15
Swartest night stretched over wretched men there.
The ocean flowing backward, came we then to the place
Aforesaid by Circe.
Here did they rites, Perimedes and Eurylochus,
And drawing sword from my hip   20
I dug the ell-square pitkin;
Poured we libations unto each the dead,
First mead and then sweet wine, water mixed with white
flour.
Then prayed I many a prayer to the sickly death's-head;
As set in Ithaca, sterile bulls of the best   25
For sacrifice, heaping the pyre with goods,
A sheep to Tiresias only, black and a bell-sheep.
Dark blood flowed in the fosse,
Souls out of Erebus, cadaverous dead, of brides
Of youths and at the old who had borne much;   30
Souls stained with recent tears, girls tender,
Men many, mauled with bronze lance heads,

Battle spoil, bearing yet dreory arms,
These many crowded about me; with shouting,
Pallor upon me, cried to my men for more beasts;   35
Slaughtered the heards, sheep slain of bronze;
Poured ointment, cried to the gods,
To Pluto the strong, and praised Proserpine;
Unsheathed the narrow sword,
I sat to keep off the impetuous impotent dead,   40
Till I should hear Tiresias.
But first Elpenor came, our friend Elpenor,
Unburied, cast on the wide earth,
Limbs that we left in the house of Circe,
Unwept, unwrapped in sepulchre, since toils urged other.
Pitiful spirit. And I cried in hurried speech:
"Elpenor, how art thou come to this dark coast?
Cam'st thou afoot, outstripping seamen?"

    And he in heavy speech:
"Ill fate and abundant wine. I slept in Circe's ingle.   50
Going down the long ladder unguarded,
I fell against the buttress,
Shattered the nape-nerve, the soul sought Avernus.
But thou, O King, I bid remember me, unwept, unburied,
Heap up mine arms, be tomb by sea-bord, and inscribed:
A man of no fortune, and with a name to come.
And set my oar up, that I swung mid fellows."

And Anticlea came, whom I beat off, and then Tiresias
Theban,
Holding his golden wand, knew me, and spoke first:
"A second time? why? man of ill star,   60
Facing the sunless dead and this joyless region?
Stand from the fosse, leave me my bloody bever
    For soothsay."
      And I stepped back,
    And he stong with the blood, said then: "Odysseus 65

Shalt return through spiteful Neptune, over dark seas,
Lose all companions." And then Anticlea came.
Lie quiet Divus. I mean, that is Andreas Divus,
In officina Wecheli, 1538, out of Homer.
And he sailed, by Sirens and thence outward and away 70
And unto Circe.
 Venerandam,
In the Creatan's phrase, with the golden crown, Aphrodite,
Cypri munimenta sortita est, mirthful, orichalchi, with golden
Girdles and breast bands, thou with dark eyelids 75
Bearing the golden bough of Argicida. So that:

- **keel**: a synecdoche for ship.
- **swart**: black, swarthy.
- **Circe**: a minor goddess, daughter of the Titan, Helio.
- **trim-coifed**: suggests a short hair style.
- **Kimmerian**: the Kimmerians, according to Homer, lived at the end of the world at the entrance to Hades.
- **Perimedes and Eurylochus**: two of Odysseus's crew members; Eurylochus was second-in-command.
- **ell-square**: an ell is a unit of measurement based on the forearm (c. 18 inches).
- **pitkin**: a small pit.
- **death's-head**: a skull.
- **Ithaca**: a Greek island; the home of Odysseus.
- **Tiresias**: a blind prophet of Apollo and fortune teller.
- **fosse**: a defensive ditch.
- **Erebus**: one of the primordial deities in Greek mythology.

- **dreory**: dreary.
- **Pluto**: the god of the underworld.
- **Proserpine**: Roman goddess of grain and agriculture.
- **Elpenor** was the youngest comrade of Odysseus. While on the island of Circe he became drunk and decided to spend the night on the roof. In the morning he slipped on the ladder fell, and broke his neck.
- **Ingle**: literally, a fireplace. Perhaps Pound is thinking of some kind of shelter on the roof near Circe's chimney.
- **Avernus**: the infernal regions.
- **Anticlea**: mother of Odysseus.
- **bever**: beverage.
- **Neptune**: Roman god of the sea.
- **Andreas Divus**: a Renaissance scholar.
- **officina Wecheli**: at the publishing world (from the title page of his edition of the book: Parisiis, In officina Christiani Wecheli, MDXXXVIII.
- **Venerandam**: veneration, reverence (for Aphrodite).
- **Cypri munimenta sortita est**: "The citadels of Cyprus were her appointed realm."
- **orichalchi**: copper.
- **Argicida** – an epithet for the god, Mercury, which means "slayer of Argos".

Before answering the questions, make sure you understand the basic story which Pound is telling. Here's what to do:

- Read *Canto I* with careful reference to the glossary.
- Read the explanation of *Canto I* in the Commentary.
- Read the translation of the original text of *The*

Odyssey, which you can find on pages 81ff.

• Finally, re-read *Canto I*.

QUESTIONS

1. What are the differences in content (the story) between Pound's translation and the translation on pp. 81ff. which closely follows the original.
2. What are the differences in language and style?
3. Why do you think Pound breaks his narrative to declare his source?
4. Why do you think he ended with a sort of hymn of praise to Aphrodite?
5. Why do you think he wrote it in the way he did? (Latin phrases mixed with English words and phrases, and obscure references to Greek mythology.
6. What is your personal interpretation of the last two words and colon?
7. Pound has used a verse-form adapted from Anglo-Saxon poetry. Revise this verse form by referring back to *The Seafarer* and the description of the metre on page 21. Then choose a section of 10-12 lines and analyse it by marking the stressed syllables and alliteration.
8. Why do you think Pound chose this verse form for his translation?
9. Find places where the alliteration emphasises the meaning.
10. Pound has deliberately chosen to use a great deal of archaic and unusual diction, for example, "swart", line 3, as well as archaic word order ("poured we", line 22), and grammar ("art thou", line 47). Find other examples, and state what effect they have.
11. Pound is said to have identified with the hero Odysseus, because he, too, has undertaken, and in his Cantos, is in process of undertaking, his own Odyssey in life and poetry. From what you know of Pound (his biography,

and his earlier poems) explore this idea as it applies to *Canto I.*

COMMENTARY

Ezra Pound's *The Cantos* is a long, incomplete, poem in 116 sections. It is considered to be one of the most important works of modernist poetry. However, it is a very difficult work, and Pound's extensive intertextuality means that it requires a reader who has at least university-level education in the humanities, a wide general knowledge, a knowledge of the main European languages, as well as Latin and Greek, a detailed knowledge of classical culture and literature, and an equally detailed knowledge of European history, literature and philosophy, as well as some knowledge of oriental language, literature and philosophy. The less well educated must rely on notes, and when the notes approach the length of the poem (as they do, above) it is tempting to throw *The Cantos* out of the window and pick up an anthology of Georgian poetry. Fortunately, we have only two Cantos to deal with, so let's get on with it!

Canto I consists primarily of Pound's translation of *Book XI* of Homer's *Odyssey*. It begins "in media res" (in the midst of action). At the end of *Book X*, Odysseus's crew convinces Odysseus to leave Circe's island and resume the journey home. Circe advises them that they first must visit Hades to consult with the spirit of the blind prophet Tiresias. The goddess offers instructions and supplies for the journey. *Book XI,* and Canto I, begin with Odysseus and his crew setting sail.

Hades is near to the land of the Kimmerians. Odysseus follows Circe's instructions. Eurylochus and Perimedes perform the appropriate rites and Odysseus digs a pit at the site prescribed and pours libations of mead, wine and water

77

mixed with flour. He says prayers then then sacrifices bulls, and a sheep to Tiresias. Many souls come out of Hades, crying for more sacrifices, but Odysseus is waiting for Tiresias. Elpenor (see note) is the first spirit to speak to Odsysseus. He explains how he died, and Odysseus will go back to Circe's island, find his body, and give it a proper burial.

Odysseus' mother, Anticleia, comes, but he pushes her away so that he can hear Tiresias. Tiresias, strengthened by the sacrificial blood, make a prophecy. This is very long in the original text (see pp. 81ff.), but Pound just gives the essence of it: Odysseus will get home to Ithaca but will lose his companions on the way because of Neptune's wrath.

Pound breaks into his translation at this point to acknowledge his source: Andreas Divus, whose Latin translation of Homer was published in 1538.

He continues his story by telling how Odysseus sails back to Circe's island (to carry out his promise to Elpenor).

The end of the Canto is obscure. It is like reading a foreign language as the many classical names and allusions and Latin quotations have to be looked up to make sense of it. It is basically Pound's tribute to the Aphrodite (the Greek goddess of love and beauty) based on a Latin text which he partly quotes and partly paraphrases. This is a simplified version of what he is saying:

> I give praise to the Aphrodite, who wears a golden crown. The cities of Cyprus are her realm. She is full of mirth, (something to do with copper), wears golden girdles and breast bands. You have dark eyelids (he switches to a direct address to the goddess), and carry Mercury's golden bough (a symbol of rebirth).

The Canto ends with the tanatalising phrase, "So that" followed by a colon, leaving the reader in suspense, thinking, " 'So that:?' – 'so what?' ". There are many ways to interpret this. Perhaps Pound is inviting the reader to reflect on the significance of what he has just written, or perhaps he is directing the reader into the next Canto. This is my preferred interpretation, as the Homerian theme is picked up in the first few lines (after an address to Robert Browning) with:

And the wave runs in the beach-groove:
"Elpenor, ελέναυς and ελέπτολις!"
        And poor old Homer blind, blind, as a bat,
Ear, ear for the sea-surge, murmur of old men's voices...

Surprisingly, Pound has chosen Anglo-Saxon alliterative verse as the metre in which to write this Canto. The original Greek text is composed in dactylic hexameters (dactyl = one stressed syllable followed by two unstressed syllables) , of which the following is an example:

I sing of arms and the man, who first from the shores of Troy

If you say the line you can hear the six stresses. However, Classical Greek is not stressed. The nature of the language means that instead of stressed and unstressed syllables, a pattern long and short vowels is used.

The *Iliad* and *Odyssey* were epic poems which were composed orally, and the English equivalent is *Beowulf* – a poem which was composed orally in the 6th or 7th century and passed on for hundreds of years before being written down. Pound decided that the metre of Anglo-Saxon oral poetry (see the description in pp. 13ff.) would be the most appropriate metre for a translation into English, and he has built on this idea by using a range of archaic diction and grammar.

We can see by comparing translations that Pound has reworked his material very freely, omitting a long section of Tiresias' prophecy, and changing many details throughout the whole extract – so much so that the word 'translation' is inappropriate: "re-working" or "re-imagining" are more accurate descriptions. Of course, when we get to the last 9 lines of the Canto, the ideas are entirely Pound's own, and put the whole of his reworking into a new perspective. It is now something personal. The hymn to Aphrodite is in Pound's own voice, and that links the experiences of Odysseus with Pound's own experiences. *The Odyssey* tells the story of Odysseus' ten-year journey home from Troy, and the word "Odyssey" has come to mean any epic journey. As with the word "journey", "Odyssey" has both a literal meaning and a figurative one. Pound's personal Odyssey is that he has gone on a long physical journey from his native America, to London, Paris, and then to Italy, in the course of which he has discovered many cultures and languages. This has informed his poetic "Odyssey" in which he began with traditional poetic forms, and was influenced by ancient cultures, as well as modernist approaches (such as Imagism). In *The Cantos*, his culminating achievement, he brings together everything he has learned. Thus, *The Cantos* is itself a sort of journey through civilisation – and what better place to start than with civilisation's first great monument – *The Odyssey* of Homer.

THE ODYSSEY, BOOK XI, THE VISIT TO THE DEAD.

Translated by Samuel Butler

Then, when we had got down to the sea shore we drew our ship into the water and got her mast and sails into her; we also put the sheep on board and took our places, weeping and in great distress of mind. Circe, that great and cunning goddess, sent us a fair wind that blew dead aft and staid steadily with us keeping our sails all the time well filled; so we did whatever wanted doing to the ship's gear and let her go as the wind and helmsman headed her. All day long her sails were full as she held her course over the sea, but when the sun went down and darkness was over all the earth, we got into the deep waters of the river Oceanus, where lie the land and city of the Cimmerians who live enshrouded in mist and darkness which the rays of the sun never pierce neither at his rising nor as he goes down again out of the heavens, but the poor wretches live in one long melancholy night.

When we got there we beached the ship, took the sheep out of her, and went along by the waters of Oceanus till we came to the place of which Circe had told us. Here Perimedes and Eurylochus held the victims, while I drew my sword and dug the trench a cubit each way. I made a drink-offering to all the dead, first with honey and milk, then with wine, and thirdly with water, and I sprinkled white barley meal over the whole, praying earnestly to the poor feckless ghosts, and promising them that when I got back to Ithaca I would sacrifice a barren heifer for them, the best I had, and would load the pyre with good things. I also particularly promised that

Teiresias should have a black sheep to himself, the best in all my flocks. When I had prayed sufficiently to the dead, I cut the throats of the two sheep and let the blood run into the trench, whereon the ghosts came trooping up from Erebus--brides, young bachelors, old men worn out with toil, maids who had been crossed in love, and brave men who had been killed in battle, with their armour still smirched with blood; they came from every quarter and flitted round the trench with a strange kind of screaming sound that made me turn pale with fear.

When I saw them coming I told the men to be quick and flay the carcasses of the two dead sheep and make burnt offerings of them, and at the same time to repeat prayers to Hades and to Proserpine; but I sat where I was with my sword drawn and would not let the poor feckless ghosts come near the blood till Teiresias should have answered my questions.

The first ghost that came was that of my comrade Elpenor, for he had not yet been laid beneath the earth. We had left his body unwaked and unburied in Circe's house, for we had had too much else to do. I was very sorry for him, and cried when I saw him: "Elpenor," said I, "how did you come down here into this gloom and darkness? You have got here on foot quicker than I have with my ship."

"Sir," he answered with a groan, "it was all bad luck, and my own unspeakable drunkenness. I was lying asleep on the top of Circe's house, and never thought of coming down again by the great staircase but fell right off the roof and broke my neck, so my soul came down to the house of Hades. And now I beseech you by all those whom you have left behind you, though they are not here, by your wife, by the father who brought you up when you were a child, and by Telemachus who is the one hope of your house, do what I shall now ask you. I know that when you leave this limbo you will again hold your ship for the Aeaean island. Do not go thence leaving me unwaked and unburied behind you, or I may bring heaven's anger upon you; but burn me with whatever armour I have, build a barrow for me on the sea shore, that may tell people in days to come what a poor unlucky fellow I was, and plant over my grave the oar I used to row with when I was yet alive and with my messmates."

And I said, "My poor fellow, I will do all that you have asked of me."

Thus, then, did we sit and hold sad talk with one another, I on the one side of the trench with my sword held over the blood, and the ghost of my comrade saying all this to me from the other side. Then came the ghost of my dead mother Anticlea, daughter to Autolycus. I had left her alive when I set out for Troy and was moved to tears when I saw her, but even so, for all my sorrow I would not let her come near the blood till I had asked my questions of Teiresias.

Then came also the ghost of Theban Teiresias, with his golden sceptre in his hand. He knew me and said, "Ulysses, noble son of Laertes, why, poor man, have you left the light of day and come down to visit the dead in this sad place? Stand back from the trench and withdraw your sword that I may drink of the blood and answer your questions truly."

So I drew back, and sheathed my sword, whereon when he had drank of the blood he began with his prophecy. "You want to know," said he, "about your return home, but heaven will make this hard for you. I do not think that you will escape the eye of Neptune, who still nurses his bitter grudge against you for having blinded his son. Still, after much suffering you may get home if you can restrain yourself and your companions when your ship reaches the Thrinacian island, where you will find the sheep and cattle belonging to the sun, who sees and gives ear to everything. If you leave these flocks unharmed and think of nothing but of getting home, you may yet after much hardship reach Ithaca; but if you harm them, then I forewarn you of the destruction both of your ship and of your men. Even though you may yourself escape, you will return in bad plight after losing all your men, in another man's ship, and you will find trouble in your house, which will be overrun by high-handed people, who are devouring your substance under the pretext of paying court and making presents to your wife."

CANTO CXVI

Came Neptunus
        his mind leaping
                like dolphins
These concepts the human mind has attained.
To make Cosmos –   5
To achieve the possible –
Muss., wrecked for an error,
But the record
        the palimpsest –
a little light   10
        in great darkness –
cuniculi –
An old "crank" dead in Virginia.
Unprepared young burdened with records,
The vision of the Madonna   15
        above the cigar butts
           and over the portal.
"Have made a mass of laws"
                (mucchio di leggi)
Litterae nihil sanantes   20
        Justinian's,
a tangle of works unfinished.
I have brought the great ball of crystal;
        who can lift it?
Can you enter the great acorn of light?   25
        But the beauty is not the madness
Tho' my errors and wrecks lie about me.
And I am not a demigod,
I cannot make it cohere.
If love be not in the house there is nothing.   30
The voice of famine unheard.
How came beauty against this blackness,
Twice beauty under the elms –

To be saved by squirrels and bluejays?
                    "plus j'aime le chien"   35
 Ariadne.
              Disney against the metaphysicals,
and Laforgue more than they thought in him,
Spire thanked me in proposito
And I have learned more from Jules   40
                        (Jules Laforgue) since then
deeps in him,
              And Linnaeus.
                        chi crescerà i nostri –
but about that terzo   45
              third heaven,
                    that Venere,
again is all "paradiso"
          a nice quiet paradise
                    over the shambles,   50
and some climbing
              before the take-off,
to "see again,"
the verb is "see," not 'walk on'
i.e. it coheres all right   55
              even if my notes do not cohere.
Many errors,
          a little rightness,
to excuse his hell
                    and my paradiso.   60
And as to why they go wrong,
                    thinking of rightness
And as to who will copy this palimpsest?
          al poco giorno
                        ed al gran cerchio d'ombra 65
But to affirm the gold thread in the pattern
                        (Torcello)
al Vicolo d'oro
          (Tigullio).

To confess wrong without losing rightness: 70
Charity I have had sometimes,
        I cannot make it flow thru.
A little light, like a rushlight
                to lead back to splendour.

- **Neptunus**: Neptune.
- **Muss**: Benito Amilcare Andrea Mussolini was the leader of the Italian Fascist Party.
- **palimpsest**: a manuscript page from which the text has been erased so that the page can be reused.
- **cuniculi**: small tunnel or drain.
- **An old "crank"**: Pound is thinking of a man who originated a theory about the origin of a giant footprint (shades of Bigfoot here!). This reminds Pound of *Ode 245* in the *Shih-ching*, where an immaculate conception is mentioned. Chian Yuan, wife of the Emperor K'u becaomes pregnant when she steps in the big toe of the footprint (was it a Yeti's?). This idea of virgin birth links into his descripiton of the Madonna image.
- **mucchio di leggi**: a haystack of laws.
- **litterae nihil sanantes**: literature which heals nothing.
- **ball of crystal/acorn of light**: imagery from Neoplatonic light philosophy.
- **"plus j'aime le chien"**: the more I loved dogs.
- **Ariadne**: in Greek mythology, Ariadne was the daughter of Minos, King of Crete. She is associated with mazes and labyrinths because of her involvement in the myth of Theseus and the Minotaur.
- **Disney**: Pound was a great fan of Disney films.
- **Laforgue**: Jules Laforgue (1860 – 1887) was a French Symbolist poet.

- **Spire**: André Spire (1868 – 1966) was a French poet, writer, and Zionist activist.
- **in proposito**: an Italian conjunction which means: with "regard to", "but", "because", "in order that".
- **chi crescerà i nostri**: a quotation from the *Divine Comedy* by Dante Alighieri, Volume 3, Paradiso. Pound (as usual) assumes that the reader knows the work so well that it does not need to be quoted in full. The full quotation is: "Ecco chi crescerà li nostri amori" (Behold the one shall increase our love).
- **Terzo**: Italian for "third".
- **Venere**: Italian for Venus.
- **al poco giorno ed al gran cerchio d'ombra**: another quotation from Dante: "But to affirm the gold thread in the pattern".
- **Torcello**: a majestic sunken city in the Venetian lagoon.
- **al Vicolo d'oro**: the Golden Lane – the beach on the Bay of Tigullio, near Rapallo, where Pound lived in 1930s.

This canto is even more obscure than *Canto I*, so the first step is to try to get some understanding of what Pound is saying. Here's what to do:

- Read *Canto CXVI* with careful reference to the glossary.
- Read the paraphrase of the Canto in the Commentary below.
- Finally, re-read *Canto CXVI*, then have a go at the following questions. When pondering the questions, always work from the original, referring to the paraphrase only for clarification.

QUESTIONS

1. How does the opening of the poem link to *Canto I?*
2. Lines 13 to 17 make a comparison between writing and the virgin birth. First, read the notes, and explain the both parts of the comparison in your own words, then consider the idea behind the comparison.
3. How do the two images "great ball of crystal" and "great acorn of light" (lines 23 -15) indicate Pound's aspirations in poetry?
4. What qualities should a great poem have, according to lines 30 – 33?
5. Where in this Canto does Pound express doubts about his own poetic achievement? What are these doubts? (Tip: look through the whole poem to collect evidence).
6. Read the notes and the paraphrase, and then explain in your own words what he means by "saved by squirrels and bluejays" (line 34).
7. What point is Pound making when he alludes to Dante's *Paradiso?*
8. He goes on to mention two places in Italy which are a sort of paradise – where are they, and what is good about them (see notes)?
9. At the end of the poem, Pound says what he needs to write the kind of poetry he aspires to. What is it, and what image does he use to describe it? How does it compare with the images in lines 23 – 25?
10. Re-read Pound's definition of a good image on page 11, then see if you can find any images in this poem which fit this definition.
11. Read the explanation of symbolist poetry in the commentary (pp. 105ff.) and say where you think this poem is primarily Symbolist or Imagist and why.

12. Comment on the verse form of this Canto.
13. Write your own "Pound Canto" (see pp. 177ff.). More than anything else, this will help you to understand how his poetry works.

COMMENTARY

Canto I was difficult enough, but this is much harder. It is highly intertextual, employing a range of allusions to classical mythology, other poets from Dante to Jules Laforgue, sprinkled with numerous quotations from Latin, Italian and French. All this is linked with phrases which suggest ideas rather than state them clearly. It is, by a long way, the hardest literary text that the author has ever had to deal with. He has researched it as best as he can (with reference to such books as: *A Companion to the Cantos of Ezra Pound*, Terrel, 1984, and *Ezra Pound's Cantos*, ed. Peter Makin, 2006) and offers the paraphrase on page 91 as the fruit of his labours.

Poetry like Pound's depends on its ambiguities and any paraphrase is likely to be very limiting as it can only give one interpretation. I apologise to the many critics who may wish to interpret this Canto differently, but if you can do it better, please do, and email me the result to include in the next edition of these notes.

PARAPHRASE OF CANTO CXVI

Neptune (as prophesied by Tiresias) helped me to get home. Neptune's mind is as lively as leaping dolphins, and some of his concepts can be achieved by the human (my?) mind.

I wanted to create a universe, but would be content if I could achieve the possible (in poetry). Mussolini attempted to achieve something, but made a mistake and was destroyed.

The historical record regarding Mussolini is bad, but there are some good things coming out of it, like a new text written over one that has been erased, or like a little light in great darkness, or small tunnels (perhaps the "palimpsest" are the Cantos that it inspired Pound to write).

There is a crazy old man in Virginia who talks about the legend of a large footprint (a Bigfoot enthusiast, perhaps?) which reminds me of a Chinese legend in which a woman gets pregnant by stepping in the toe of such a footprint (of a Yeti?). That reminds me of a Madonna image I have seen over a church portal which represents something wonderful (the virgin birth) though the area in front of it was littered with cigar butts. (Pound seems to be talking about poetic inspiration arising from nothing, like a virgin birth).

The Roman emperor, Justinian, wrote a pile of laws as big as a haystack, but that was literature which didn't do much good because the laws did not prevent the ultimate fall of the Roman Empire. It was a tangle of unfinished work.

I too am trying to achieve something great: to represent the universe in poetry. My project is like trying to find truth by gazing into a crystal ball. It looks like a large acorn full of light, but I can't enter it, can you?

There is a degree of madness in my ideas (perhaps because I really am insane), but beauty cannot be found in madness. I have made many mistakes (in life and in poetry), and as I am not a demigod I cannot make my ideas work. I know that there must be beauty in my poetry; and pity, like the pity inspired by listening to the cries of those who are starving, but how can I reconcile beauty and suffering?

While sitting under some elms trees I had two visions of beauty: squirrels and bluejays. It seems strange to say it, but they saved me by showing me the way to develop my art. Indeed, I love my dogs more and more (because they also show me natural beauty).

Finding the way to go in poetry is like negotiating Ariadne's labyrinth, or balancing Disney's films against the metaphysical poets (Disney is easy to understand but superficial; the metaphyiscal poets are difficult to understand but profound). For example, Andre Spire thanked me for my efforts, and I learned a great deal from the profundity of the symbolist poetry of Jules Laforgue and Linnaeus (?).

I also learned from Dante's *Inferno* about the one (Jesus) who shall increase our love. But with reference to the third heaven described by Dante in his *Paradiso* which is the sphere of Venus. I can see it and it is my goal. It will take some effort before I can see it clearly – I want to emphasise that I am talking about seeing it and writing about it, not actually walking there!

That idea works out, even though my notes for my poems are incoherent and are full of errors. However, I got a few things right, and that excuses the hellish muddle of the rest. What I got right was the vision of Paradise, but I don't know why my writing sometimes goes wrong, when I know what would be right. I feel as though I am trying to draw a huge circle (of light?) in the small hours of darkness, and to find the gold thread in a (complex) pattern, such as I have seen in Torcello, the sunken city of Venice, and on the Golden Road (the beach) at Tigullio (near Rapello, where Pound lived in the 1930's).

How can I admit my mistakes without it spoiling what I have done right? I cannot make the ideas flow, but just a little inspiration, like a rushlight, will lead me to write splendid poetry (but it will be far from the poetry I aspire to, just as a rushlight is very dim compared to "a great acorn of light").

COMMENTARY CONTINUED

This is that last Canto that Pound finished, but it is not the last he had planned. As can be seen in this Canto, he had severe doubts about the quality of his work, and felt unable to continue. However, he left notes for four more Cantos.

Nevertheless, there is a sense of completion in this Canto, as Odysseus, now clearly identified with the poet, comes home and no longer fears Neptune, but is inspired by his lively mind.

Through a series of symbols, images and allusions, Pound describes his ambitions in poetry: to represent the universe (Cosmos), but he doubts that he has the ability to do it. He fears that his poems are just a tangled mess, full of errors, and that he cannot make it work ("cohere"). He recognises that love, pity and beauty are essential qualities for his poetry, and nature (elms, bluejays, squirrels, dogs) helps him. He pays tribute to the poets he has learned from, and uses an allusion to Dante's *Paradiso* to describe the paradise he is aiming for. He knows he will never "walk" there, but at least he can "see" it. He refers to two beautiful places in Italy that have given him a glimpse of Paradise (Torcello and Tigullio). He ends by saying how difficult he finds it to make his poetry sound "right" and to "flow", but even a little inspiration ("rushlight") will help him to achieve something, even though it can never be as great as his vision. This is emphasised by the comparison of the image of the rushlight with the images of the "great ball of crystal" and the "great acorn of light".

The style of this Canto is primarily symbolist. Symbolist poets such as Arthur Rimbaud, Stéphane Mallarmé and Jules Laforgue rejected conventional figures of speech such as metaphor, personification, and simile, especially the latter, because of its literal, logical words of comparison (like/as) in favour of grand, illogical, intuitive associations which consisted of mythological allusions, references to other authors, people (famous and infamous), places, and a wide range of other symbols. Key symbols in this Canto are: Nepture, the Cosmos, Mussolini, Bigfoot, the Madonna, Justinian's laws, the Neoplatonic symbols of the ball of crystal and the acorn of light, elms, squirrels, bluejays and dogs, Ariadne, Disney, French symbolist poets, Dante's Paradiso, Torcello, Tigullio, and a rushlight.

There is nothing in this poem to compare with the powerful Imagist imagery of *In a Station of the Metro*.

The verse form is free verse set out in units of speech, or ideas which are so strong that it would (almost) be possible to reconstruct the line layout if it had been set out like prose. Each line break emphasises an idea, symbol or allusion.

THEMES

	AUTOBIOGRAPHY	CONVENTIONALITY/ MATERIALISM	CULTURE/CIVILISATION/ POETRY	JOURNEY	LOVE	WAR
Portrait d'une femme	*	*	*			
The Seafarer			*	*		
The Garden		*	*			
Salutation		*	*			
Salutation the Second		*	*			
Commission		*	*			
The Bath Tub	*				*	
In a Station of the Metro			*		*	
The River-Merchant's Wife: a Letter			*	*	*	
Lament of the Frontier Guard; The City of Choan			*			*
Hugh Selwyn Mauberley (parts IV and V).	*	*	*			*
Canto I	*		*	*		
Canto CXVI	*		*		*	

TABLE OF THEMES IN THIS SELECTION

Themes are slippery things as different readers will identify different themes in the same text, or the same themes but give them different names. After much consideration, the author believes that six main themes can be identified in this selection. These are shown in the above table. Taking Pound's works, as a whole, other important themes can be identified, for example, he has a great deal to say about commerce, banking and money, though there is very little on this subject in this selection. It has also been argued that a Neo-Platonic philosophy underlies many poems, though this applies only to *Canto CXVI* in our selection.

AUTOBIOGRAPHY

The main part of *Canto I* is a translation of the *Odyssey*. We know from subsequent sections of *The Cantos* that Pound identified himself with Odysseus, thus *The Cantos* are partly autobiographical. They also tell the story of his poetic journey – the quest to which he has dedicated his life. In *Drafts and Fragments of Cantos CX–CXVII* he expresses his sense of failure to achieve this quest:

I lost my center
        fighting the world.
The dreams clash
        and are shattered—
that I tried to make a paradiso
                terrestre

But despite this latter day disillusionment, the general critical opinion is that Pound "is a central figure in the development of modern English poetry" (Michael Alexander, 1988). His assessment at the end of *Canto CXVI* is probably more accurate – that he aspired to a "great acorn of light" and achieved a "rushlight" – but that "rushlight" is a considerable achievement.

Pound's poetic development can be traced even in this limited selection, beginning with his *Portrait d'une Femme*, written in traditional blank verse (iambic pentameter). The Seafarer shows what he learned from translation, and his later translations of Japanese and particularly Chinese poems would teach him much more. The influence of the Imagist movement can be seen in several poems, particularly in *In A Station of the Metro*. By the time he wrote *Mauberley*, Pound was moving on from Imagism, and writing in a style that could be described as modernist. In *The Cantos*, all his poetic experience comes together, and they are written in a multiplicity of styles, though perhaps overall, they could be described as Vorticist. A more detailed account of Pound's poetic styles can be found in the next chapter.

Pound's complete works contain a great deal of autobiographical material, especially *The Cantos*, but there is not much of it in our selection. The vivid description in *Portrait d'un Femme* suggests that he is referring to a woman he knew. This could also be true of the woman in *The Garden*, though she could just be a "type" – the typical bourgeoise whom he frequently criticises. *The Bath Tub* possibly gives us a glimpse into Pound's private life, though he is more interested in the image that describes her than the woman or their relationship. *Hugh Edwin Mauberley* is about a poet whose life has become empty and meaningless, whom many critics believe is Pound. The poem is therefore strongly autobiographical. However, Parts IV and V are mainly about WWI, and are autobiographical only in that they show Pound's very emotional reaction to the war.

The autobiographical element in *Canto I* only becomes apparent when we read subsequent Cantos. *Canto CXVI* seems to complete the "Odyssey" as it has a sense of homecoming. However, it is mainly about Pound's poetry rather than his life.

CONVENTIONALITY/MATERIALISM

Pound was fighting conventionality all his life. His rebellious attitude prevented him from finishing his PhD, and got him fired from his first job (see page 2). However, it was also the basis for his rejection of traditional poetry and led him to experiment with different forms of modernism.

His most powerful attack on conventionality and materialism can be seen in his book, *Lustra* (1916) where he attacks the attitude of the conventional middle-class bourgeois citizen. He sees them is being false (*Portrait d'une Femme)*, over-sensitive and bored with their lives (*The Garden*), smug, yet unhappy (*Salutation*), imprisoned by the "dead hand" of convention, and sexually frustrated (*Commission*). In this poem he gives a long list of the problems they suffer from and expresses the hope that his poetry will help to liberate them – the stance of a typical left-leaning bohemian poet.

However, his views about materialism began to change as he focused on the capitalist economic system and international finance. In *Mauberley*, he uses the term "usury" for the first time, and later developed this these ideas in T*he Cantos* in a way that has led him to the accusation of anti-Semitism.

It is ironic that the former bohemian poet became a mouthpiece for Fascism and anti-Semitisim during WWII, though we should not forget that he repudiated these views towards the end of his life (see page 5).

CULTURE/CIVILISATION/POETRY

Pound's ability to speak nine European languages gave him a profound knowledge of European literature and culture. Later, he added a knowledge of Japanese and Chinese language and culture. This broad knowledge infuses all his work and is the basis of his extensive intertextuality. In this small syllabus selection, we are introduced to the worlds of France, Italy, Anglo-Saxon England, Classical Greek mythology, and the China of the Tang Dynasty. *The Cantos*, in particular, are a "vortex" of cultural references from a vast array of cultures and languages, and important works of European literature such as *The Odyssey*, Dante's *Divine Comedy*, French Symbolist poetry, and classic Chinese poetry. It is interesting to compare this with the parochial outlook of the Georgian poets, of which Blunden's *Winter, East Anglia* is a typical example.

This celebration of European culture turned sour during WWI. When it seemed to many that the culmination of centuries of cultural development had led only to carnage on an industrial scale. His most powerful expression of this disillusionment in this selection is in *Mauberley* where he describes it as "a botched civilization".

For Pound, the most important aspect of civilisation and culture was poetry. This was his great project in life (see pages 97-98), and he wanted to learn as much as he could from the poets of every country and culture.

JOURNEY

Three poems in this selection deal vividly with the theme of journey. *The Seafarer* is a translation, so the ideas expressed in it are not Pound's. Once again, he is more interested in the language than the theme. However, we know from *The Cantos* that he was interested in this theme as he saw it as representing a) his own poetic journey, and b) his, and every human being's personal journey through life. Re-read the commentary on this poem and consider how far the ideas about journey, life, suffering, exile, etc., have a general application.

The River Merchant's Wife uses the motif of journey to highlight the poem's major theme of love. See the commentary on this poem to see how both themes are expressed.

Pound's most powerful treatment of the theme of journey is in *Canto I*, where he identified his personal and poetic journey with Odysseus' long journey of return from Tory to Ithaca. In *Canto CXVI* there is a sense that this journey has been completed.

LOVE

Pound is not a love poet, and the most powerful love poem in this selection, *The River Merchant's Wife*, is a translation from Chinese. The power with which love is expressed in that poem is detailed in the commentary on page 47. *The Bath Tub*, if it is an autobiographical poem, and not primarily an experiment in imagery, suggests a somewhat cynical attitude to love which is reflected in a comment he made about having been in Paris for three months and not found a mistress. In *Canto CXVI*, he acknowledges the importance of human love in the line "if love be not in the house there is nothing", though as he is talking about his poetry in this part of the canto, "house" could refer to poetry rather than to his personal life. On the other hand, this reference can be seen as part of a mystical philosophy of love, connected with the Neoplatonist philosophy that he develops in *The Cantos*.

CHRIS WEBSTER

WAR

Like many people of his generation, Pound experienced bitter disillusionment at the great loss of life in Word War I, and he wrote vividly about his feelings, particularly in *Mauberley* and *The Cantos*. He was similarly outraged by the World War II, which he wrote about in the so-called "Pisan Cantos" (*Cantos LXXIV – LXXXIV*). However, unlike Wilfred Owen and Siegfried Sasson, he did not fight at the front, and his poetry consists mainly of ideas and abstractions. Ironically, it is Wilfred Owen who comes closer to Pound's own poetic aims in *Dulce et Decorum Est* (see p. 70). Furthermore, Pound's poetry on WWII is tainted by his anti-Semitism, and his support for the Fascists. To put it simply, if it is war poetry you are interested in, other poets do it better.

STYLES

	IMAGIST	MODERNIST	SYMBOLIST	TRADITIONAL	TRANSLATION	VORTICIST
Portrait d'une femme				*		
The Seafarer					*	
The Garden	*	*				
Salutation		*				
Salutation the Second		*				
Commission		*				
The Bath Tub	*	*				
In a Station of the Metro	*	*				
The River-Merchant's Wife: a Letter	*	*			*	
Lament of the Frontier Guard; The City of Choan	*	*			*	
Hugh Selwyn Mauberley (parts IV and V).		*				
Canto I		*	*		*	*
Canto CXVI		*	*			*

TABLE OF STYLES IN THIS SELECTION

IMAGIST

The following is a statement of the Imagist movement's aims, written by Pound and published in the Imagist magazine, *Poetry*, in 1913:

1.   Direct treatment of the 'thing', whether subjective or objective.
2.   To use absolutely no word that does not contribute to the presentation.
3.   As regarding rhythm: to compose in sequence of the musical phrase, not in sequence of the metronome.

However, clear these statements were to Imagist poets, they need further explanation today:

1.   Avoid the vague abstractions that were characteristic of Georgian poetry (Georgian poetry was the mainstream style of poetry in the early 20th century. It is sometimes described as a second-rate continuation of Victorian poetry).
2.   Write with economy of language and avoid excess verbiage.
3.   Write in free verse.

Pound's definition of the image was "that which presents an intellectual and emotional complex in an instant of time."

His discovery of Japanese and Chinese poetry helped him to refine his concept of Imagism by demonstrating how an idea, and the images that elucidates it can be juxtaposed without any grammatical links, leaving the reader to work out the connection – a technique called *parataxis*.

MODERNIST

Modernists in all the arts wanted to break with the past, rejecting literary traditions that seemed outmoded and worn out. To take one example, the dominant metre in English verse had been the iambic pentameter since the time of Geoffrey Chaucer (c.1343-1400) – which is why Pound proclaimed in *Canto LXXXI* (see page i): "to break the pentameter, that was the first heave" – but only the first; there was a lot more that seemed outmoded. Similar changes were taking place in the other arts: Pablo Picasso in painting, Igor Stravinsky in music, and Le Corbusier in architecture. Artists and writers found support in the various modernist movements that emerged in the early years of the 20th century: Constructivism, Futurism, Imagism, Surrealism, Symbolism and Vorticism, to name but a few. The horrors of the First World War only served to increase the desire of artists to distance themselves from a culture which had produced such catastrophe.

SYMBOLIST

Symbolists believed that art should represent truths that could only be described indirectly by writing in a manner that gave particular images or objects a symbolic meaning. The aims of the symbolist movement were stated by Jean Moréas in *Le Figaro* on 18th September 1886. He named Charles Baudelaire (1821-1867), Stéphane Mallarmé (1842-1898), and Paul Verlaine (1844-1896) as the three leading poets of the movement. Moréas announced that symbolism was hostile to "plain meanings, declamations, false sentimentality and matter-of-fact description". The symbolist poets wished to liberate versification from traditional rhyme and metre in order to allow greater room for "fluidity", and therefore favoured free verse.

TRADITIONALIST

Traditionalist poetry is a style of writing that developed in the 600 years since Chaucer and others introduced European versification into the English language (displacing the native alliterative style). Its features are accentual-syllabic metre (lines measures by the number of syllables and the number of stresses), the most common being the iambic pentameter ("iambic" is a poetic "foot" with an unstressed followed by a stressed syllable; "pentameter" meaning that there are five such stresses in a line) and rhyme – a device that is not well suited to the English language because the great variety of word endings leads to a paucity of rhymes. "Traditional" also refers to a range of set forms, the most common of which are the sonnet and blank verse. The word also refers to language and style. Basically, a poem, even if not strictly grammatical, has to make sense. The figurative language used draw upon a range of techniques developed over many centuries, and includes the familiar list of allusion, metaphor, personification, simile, etc. In summary, readers familiar with the great poets of the English literary tradition would find themselves within their comfort zone.

Traditional poetry continued to be popular well into the 20th century and enjoyed a large readership (see the chapter on Georgian Poetry, pp. 123ff.). However, the leading poets of the age believed that traditional poetry was worn out and had become little more than a recycling of tired cliches. The the challenge for them, in the words of Ezra Pound was to "make it new".

TRANSLATION

In 1905, Pound began an MA degree in Romance Languages at the University of Pennsylvania. During this period he claimed to have learned nine European languages. He developed a particular interest in translation, particularly the translation of poetry. Indeed, Pound's translations represent a substantial part of his work, and include translations from Homer, Anglo-Saxon, Egyptian, Chinese, Japanese, Italian (especially Dante), French (especially Provençal poetry), and Latin (the poems of Sextus Propertius, among others). Pound saw translation as the creation of an original work, and often sacrificed literal accuracy for poetic effect – an approach that annoyed many scholars.

There is no doubt that Pound's translations had an important influence on his own poetry. His experience of Japanese and Chinese poetry helped him to refine his Imagist techniques, and his Cantos are packed with allusions to other cultures, and contain fragments of many languages. It also helped him to understand the very essence of poetry, as that was the element that could never be translated.

VORTICIST

Vorticism was a modernist movement in British art of the early 20th century which contained its manifesto and the movement's rejection of representative art in favour of a geometric style tending towards abstraction. A notable figure in the movement was the English painter Wyndham Lewis (18 November 1882 – 7 March 1957) whose portrait of Pound can be seen on the cover of this book.

Pound and others wanted to adapt their ideas for poetry, and the following statement gives an idea of what they attempted: "The image is a radiant node or cluster; it is what I can, and must perforce, call a VORTEX, from which, and through which, and into which, ideas are constantly rushing." It is easy to see how this idea at work in Pound's Cantos. Even the arrangement of lines on the page in many of the cantos has a Vortex-like appearance.

POUND'S ADVICE TO POETS

1.   Pay no attention to the criticism of men who have never themselves written a notable work. Consider the discrepancies between the actual writing of the Greek poets and dramatists, and the theories of the Graeco-Roman grammarians, concocted to explain their metres.

2.   Use no superfluous word, no adjective which does not reveal something.

3.   Don't use such an expression as 'dim lands of peace'. It dulls the image. It mixes an abstraction with the concrete. It comes from the writer's not realizing that the natural object is always the adequate symbol.

4.   Go in fear of abstractions. Do not retell in mediocre verse what has already been done in good prose. Don't think any intelligent person is going to be deceived when you try to shirk all the difficulties of the unspeakably difficult art of good prose by chopping your composition into line lengths.

5.   What the expert is tired of today the public will be tired of tomorrow. Don't imagine that the art of poetry is any simpler than the art of music, or that you can please the expert before you have spent at least as much effort on the art of verse as an average piano teacher spends on the art of music.

6.   Be influenced by as many great artists as you can, but have the decency either to acknowledge the debt outright, or to try to conceal it. Don't allow 'influence' to mean merely that you mop up the particular decorative vocabulary of some one or two poets whom you happen to admire. A Turkish war correspondent was recently caught red-handed babbling in his dispatches of 'dove-grey' hills, or else it was 'pearl-pale', I can not remember.

7.   Use either no ornament or good ornament.

8.   Let the candidate fill his mind with the finest

cadences he can discover, preferably in a foreign language, so that the meaning of the words may be less likely to divert his attention from the movement; e.g. Saxon charms, Hebridean Folk Songs, the verse of Dante, and the lyrics of Shakespeare – if he can dissociate the vocabulary from the cadence. Let him dissect the lyrics of Goethe coldly into their component sound values, syllables long and short, stressed and unstressed, into vowels and consonants.

9.   It is not necessary that a poem should rely on its music, but if it does rely on its music that music must be such as will delight the expert.

10.   Let the neophyte know assonance and alliteration, rhyme immediate and delayed, simple and polyphonic, as a musician would expect to know harmony and counterpoint and all the minutiae of his craft. No time is too great to give to these matters or to any one of them, even if the artist seldom have need of them.

11.   Don't imagine that a thing will 'go' in verse just because it's too dull to go in prose.

12.   Don't be 'viewy' – leave that to the writers of pretty little philosophic essays. Don't be descriptive; remember that the painter can describe a landscape much better than you can, and that he has to know a deal more about it.

13.   When Shakespeare talks of the 'Dawn in russet mantle clad' he presents something which the painter does not present. There is in this line of his nothing that one can call description; he presents.

14.   Consider the way of the scientists rather than the way of an advertising agent for a new soap. The scientist does not expect to be acclaimed as a great scientist until he has discovered something. He begins by learning what has been discovered already. He goes from that point onward. He does not bank on being a charming fellow personally. He does not expect his friends to applaud the results of his freshman class work. Freshmen in poetry are unfortunately

not confined to a definite and recognizable class room. They are 'all over the shop'. Is it any wonder 'the public is indifferent to poetry?'

15.   Don't chop your stuff into separate iambs. Don't make each line stop dead at the end and then begin every next line with a heave. Let the beginning of the next line catch the rise of the rhythm wave, unless you want a definite longish pause. In short, behave as a musician, a good musician, when dealing with that phase of your art which has exact parallels in music. The same laws govern, and you are bound by no others.

16.   Naturally, your rhythmic structure should not destroy the shape of your words, or their natural sound, or their meaning. It is improbable that, at the start, you will he able to get a rhythm-structure strong enough to affect them very much, though you may fall a victim to all sorts of false stopping due to line ends, and caesurae.

17.   The Musician can rely on pitch and the volume of the orchestra. You can not. The term harmony is misapplied in poetry; it refers to simultaneous sounds of different pitch. There is, however, in the best verse a sort of residue of sound which remains in the ear of the hearer and acts more or less as an organ-base.

18.   A rhyme must have in it some slight element of surprise if it is to give pleasure, it need not be bizarre or curious, but it must be well used if used at all.

19.   That part of your poetry which strikes upon the imaginative eye of the reader will lose nothing by translation into a foreign tongue; that which appeals to the ear can reach only those who take it in the original.

20.   Consider the definiteness of Dante's presentation, as compared with Milton's rhetoric. Read as much of Wordsworth as does not seem too unutterably dull. If you want the gist of the matter go to Sappho, Catullus, Villon, Heine when he is in the vein, Gautier when he is not too frigid; or, if you have not the tongues, seek out the leisurely

Chaucer. Good prose will do you no harm, and there is good discipline to be had by trying to write it.

21.   Translation is likewise good training, if you find that your original matter 'wobbles' when you try to rewrite it. The meaning of the poem to be translated can not 'wobble'.

22.   If you are using a symmetrical form, don't put in what you want to say and then fill up the remaining vacuums with slush.

23.   Don't mess up the perception of one sense by trying to define it in terms of another. This is usually only the result of being too lazy to find the exact word. To this clause there are possibly exceptions

ESSAY AND EXAMINATION QUESTIONS

1.   What did Pound learn from his translation of *The Seafarer* that influenced his later poetry? Compare this with the influence of Japanese and Chinese poetry.

2.   Compare and contrast *Portrait d'une Femme* and *The Garden* with particular attention to verse form, style, imagery and the theme of conventionality/materialism, especially the attitude of the bourgeoise woman.

3.   Consider *Salutation*, *Salutation the Second* and *Commission* and examine how these poems explore the theme of conventionality/materialism. Pay particular attention to language, style and verse form.

4.   Explain Imagism with particular reference to *The Bath Tub* and *In a Station of the Metro*. Go on to examine how Pound uses Imagist techniques in his other poetry.

5.   What does Pound have to say about the theme of Love in *The River-Merchant's Wife: a Letter*, and *Canto CXVI*? What different poetic techniques is he using in these poems?

6.   With reference to *In a Station of the Metro*, *The River-Merchant's Wife: a Letter*, and *Lament of The Frontier Guard* and *The City of Choan*, examine the characteristics that Pound admired in Chinese poetry.

7.   What does Pound have to say about the theme of war in *Lament of The Frontier Guard*, *The City of Choan*, and *Hugh Selwyn Mauberley* (Parts Iv And V)? Consider the very different poetic techniques used in these poems and their

effect on the way the theme is presented.

9. Consider how the theme of "journey" is presented in *Cantos I* and *CXVI*. In what sense can these cantos be considered the beginning and the ending of a personal and poetic journey?

10. Pound shows great interest in the concept of civilisation, and related matters such as culture, language art and literature. Examine what he has to say about civilisation, including the extreme negativity expressed in *Mauberley*.

11. Compare and contrast Pound's translation of an extract from the *Odyssey* in Canto 1 with his translation of the *Seafarer*.

12. In what sense can *Cantos I* and *CXVI.* be described as "Symbolist" poetry?

13. The length of notes needed to make sense of each canto is longer than the cantos themselves – does this suggest a shortcoming in Pound's poetry, or is it a tribute to their complexity and subtlety of meaning?

14. Trace the development of Pound's poetic techniques, from the traditional poetry in *Ripostes*, to the *Vorticism* of *The Cantos*. Consider both style and verse form in your answer. Refer also, to what Pound wrote about poetry.

15. Read Pound's *Advice to Poets* on p. 109, and discuss how far he has followed his own advice.

16. Explore how Pound makes use of classic mythology from many cultures (Ancient Greece and Rome, Japan and China, historical European, Anglo-Saxon). In

your opinion, does this diversity enrich his poetry, or tend towards incoherence?

17. Georgian poetry had a wide readership. Modernist poetry is hardly read at all. Is Pound's poetry too complex, intellectual and obscure to give pleasure to the general reader?

18. Examine the role of aesthetic beauty in Pound's poems.

19. In *Canto LXXXI* (see page i), Pound wrote "To break the pentameter, that was the first heave". What did he mean by this, and what techniques did he use to do it? What else in traditional prosody did he "break", and to what effect?

20. Write about one of the following themes as presented in this selection of Pound's work: autobiography, conventionality/materialism, culture/civilisation/ poetry, journey, love, war.

21. In *Canto CLXXII*, Pound wrote of "the eternal war between light and mud". Some critics have related this to his Cantos. In other words, that there are moments of great clarity and poetic power, but a great deal of confusion. Explore this idea yourself with reference to *Cantos I* and *CXVI*..

22. Read the description of Vorticism on page 107 and consider the extent to which Pound's poetry can be considered Vorticist.

23. Re-read the definition of parataxis on p 43, then examine how Pound has used it in his poetry. Explain why this technique is valuable in Imagist poetry and give

examples from this selection.

24.   "Though Pound was reluctant to say so in public, the Cantos have a certain aspect of mediumship, as if a poem were a séance through which the voices of the dead could reverberate among the living" (Albright, 1999). Explore this idea with reference to *Cantos I* and *CXVI*.

25.   Give examples of intertextuality in Pound's poetry and examine how it enhances his communicative power.

26.   Try to identify more themes, sub-themes and motifs in Pound's work, add them to the table on page 96 then write essays about them.

27.   Write a new introduction to this selection of Pound's poems, including such topics as style (Imagism, Symbolism, influence of Chinese poetry, etc), themes (see list on page 96), and verse form.

WRITE YOUR OWN CANTO

Poetry as complex as Pound's cannot be reduced to a formula – or perhaps it can, but the result will be a far cry from the profundity of the original. The point of doing it is to experiment with some of Pound's techniques and thereby gain a better understanding of the way his poetry works.

Your poem will be primarily autobiographical. Think of an episode in your life that parallels (however loosely) an incident in classical mythology. Find a translation of that myth online, and play about with it, to make it your own, then adapt it in the follow ways:

1. If it is prose, break it up into free verse lines.

2. Adapt it to emphasise the parallels your own life.

3. Change some of the words and phrases to make them more powerful

4. Write some short, free verse reflections on your experiences – the more disconnected the better.

5. Spice them up with some quotations from foreign language poets. Anything from Dante or Goethe, or anything French is good.

6. If you speak another language, write an extended section in that language (as Pound did in some of his cantos).

7. Be intertextual! – Add a few quotations from poems or pop songs that seem relevant (or better still, irrelevant).

8. Write three or four words that sum up your experiences and type them into Google Translate set to give Chinese characters. Pound uses Chinese characters in some of his cantos.

9. Throw in a line from a haiku – a nature image or seasonal indicator (kigo) works well.

10. Throw in a few allusions to famous people and places, past and present, e.g., Julius Caesar, Marilyn Monroe, Martin Luther King, Byzantium, Bali, White Beach, Boracay.

11. Mention a Greek god or goddess.

12. Avoid similes. Avoid too much linking language. Instead, place ideas, symbols, allusions, next to each other and let the reader work out the link (parataxis!).

13. End in the middle of something. For example, Pound's *Canto I* ends, "So that:" and another Canto ends "And".

14. For the reader's sake, add notes!

Finally, you don't have to include all of the above – indeed, it would be a real mess if you did! Just start, and go with the flow.

Here is an example written by the author:

CANTO

Angela came
golden-haired
I saw her in the Uffizi
> *It's a poem of our love that doesn't rhyme**
But it was the love that didn't rhyme.

I wrote her a sonnet
but **the sonnet is broken***;
Super Antiquas Vias
at school (St Peter's, York)
> *My parents kept me from children who were rough**
Her skin was smooth as alabaster
as another Venus in the Louvre
> *(though without any bits missing*)*

**The pentameter
is disregarded, and rhyme is derided
though not by me** –
> *(O faded flower, you too are cast aside!*)*
I wrote poetry;
he had a Norton Commando
and a leather jacket –

> *"Is she really going out with him?*
> *"Well, there she is, Let's ask her"*
> *"Betty, is that Jimmy's ring you're wearing?"*
> *"Mm-mm"*
> *"Gee, it must be great riding with him"*
> *"Is he picking you up after school today?"*
> *"Mm-mm"*
> *"By the way, where did you meet him?"**

But it was not because I wrote faux-Shakespearian sonnets
> *(I was the wildest of her sonneteers*

119

and rhymed deliriously her charms eterne*)
The Swan wrote 154
and he had a "dark mistress" –
but I am just an amateur – a crow –
plenty of rhyme but no poetry –
    an amateur in love too –
    "You get the picture?"
    "Yes, we see"*
but would be more,
and I was when I met Sarah,
my *Rokeby Venus*
        Me gustaría pintar come Velazquez* –
    but I can't
        So instead
        I'll kiss the beauties that I said
        I'd like to paint.*

I met her at Tiffany's.
She out-Angelad Angela
and I had a Triumph Spitfire (Mk III).
And so I have decided
to be a modernist and write like Pound –
but what does that mean?
Drop the rhyme and write like this?
    Neuere Poeten tun viel Wasser in die Tinte*
and drop the metre for natural sound
and try instead a Canto paradigm?
Also to drop the morality of
    the thoroughly smug
    and thoroughly uncomfortable*
        ผมรักคุณ Namtai ดวยหัวใจทงหมดของฉนi*

Of course, it will be hard to understand
for those who are *enslaved-by-convention**
like Pound's *Cantos,* **being full of French**
and Italian quotations.

This poem,
(Immature poets imitate; mature poets steal*)
is **packed with obscure allusions**
to grandstand my erudition,
and Chinese translations like this one
from the *Shi Ching**:

玉 女 帶

(jade – woman – strip)

There is a woman as fine as jade.
"Slowly, and strip, strip my clothes!"
"Do not touch my silk breast-cloth!"

I didn't.

How's it hanging?" Kyra asks and now I think I'm
blushing.
It's just an expression, but jeez!*

That's what I'll do – I'll overcomplicate my poems,
like Pound,
Then who will know they're second rate?

As for Namtai
she taught me
what my school
and 50 years of life in the west
had failed to teach me
about
compassion,
mindfulness
and love
but she had never heard of Ambrosia Creamed Rice*

NOTES

- Khadija Rupa.
- The text in bold is an embedded poem.
- "Upon ancient roads" – the motto of St Peter's School, York (to set the record straight, I went to Swinton Comprehensive School with "children who were rough").
- From a poem by Stephen Spender.
- From my narrative poem *Sex and Sensibility*.
- After a haiku by Chiyo.
- *Leader of the Pack* sung by the Shangri-La's in 1965.
- From my *Ballade to Angela*.
- Peter Porter.
- *Leader of the Pack*.
- Courtesy of Google Translate: "I'd like to paint like Velazquez".
- From one of my Rondeaux, *I'd Like to Paint*.
- Johann Wolfgang von Goethe: "More recent poets put a lot of water in the ink".
- *Salutation*, Pound.
- "I love you, Namtai, with all my heart".
- *Commission*, Pound.
- T. S. Eliot.
- *The Book of Odes*, Chinese traditional.
- Barry Lyga, *The Astonishing Adventures of Fanboy and Goth Girl*.
- From my poem, *Ambrosia Creamed Rice*.

Author's note: the best thing in this poem is the line of poetry in the three Chinese characters. You can see the elegant femininity of the woman in the second character – and as for the third – it's almost a moving image of an elaborate striptease!

GEORGIAN POETRY

Georgian poetry got its name from a series of anthologies entitled *Georgian Poetry* edited by Edward Marsh between 1911 and 1922. The poets included Edmund Blunden, Rupert Brooke, Robert Graves, D. H. Lawrence, Walter de la Mare, Siegfried Sassoon and many others. The poets considered themselves modern, if not modernist, though they continued the literary traditions of the 19th century. It is this kind of poetry that modernists like Ezra Pound and T. S. Eliot were reacting against.

It is interesting that Georgian poetry enjoyed a wide readership, whereas modernist poetry appealed to a limited avant-garde – which is hardly surprising in view of the fact that much of it can be very hard to understand. Perhaps the main achievement of the modernist movement in all the arts is to alienate the general public. Instead of opera, the majority now prefer musicals, instead of orchestral concerts, pop, rock (and even – horror of horrors – rap) is preferred, and as for poetry – it is completely dead. Nobody buys poetry books these days except to study them for examinations. What is needed is a new poetry movement that is not elitist and intellectual and which appeals to ordinary people. Indeed, a few attempts have been made, for example, the Beat Poetry movement in 1950's America, and the Pop Poetry movement in 1960's Britain. The author of these notes also made an attempt (see p. 130). Perhaps one of the students reading this might want to try it for the 21st century.

Read the following examples of Georgian poetry and compare and contrast them with Pound's poetry. Also, use them as a basis for a discussion of the ideas above.

THE LISTENERS

By Walter De La Mare (1873-1956)

'Is there anybody there?' said the Traveller,
   Knocking on the moonlit door;
And his horse in the silence champed the grasses
   Of the forest's ferny floor:
And a bird flew up out of the turret,   5
   Above the Traveller's head:
And he smote upon the door again a second time;
   'Is there anybody there?' he said.
But no one descended to the Traveller;
   No head from the leaf-fringed sill   10
Leaned over and looked into his grey eyes,
   Where he stood perplexed and still.
But only a host of phantom listeners
   That dwelt in the lone house then
Stood listening in the quiet of the moonlight   15
   To that voice from the world of men:
Stood thronging the faint moonbeams on the dark stair,
   That goes down to the empty hall,
Hearkening in an air stirred and shaken
   By the lonely Traveller's call.   20
And he felt in his heart their strangeness,
   Their stillness answering his cry,
While his horse moved, cropping the dark turf,
   'Neath the starred and leafy sky;
For he suddenly smote on the door, even   25
   Louder, and lifted his head:—
'Tell them I came, and no one answered,
   That I kept my word,' he said.
Never the least stir made the listeners,
   Though every word he spake   30
Fell echoing through the shadowiness of the still house
   From the one man left awake:

Ay, they heard his foot upon the stirrup,
  And the sound of iron on stone,
And how the silence surged softly backward,   35
  When the plunging hoofs were gone.

WINTER: EAST ANGLIA,

By Edmund Charles Blunden (1871-1951)

In a frosty sunset
So fiery red with cold
The footballers' onset
Rings out glad and bold;
Then boys from daily tether   5
With famous dogs at heel
In starlight meet together
And to farther hedges steal;
Where the rats are pattering
In and out the stacks,   10
Owls with hatred chattering
Swoop at the terriers' backs.
And, frost forgot, the chase grows hot
Till a rat's a foolish prize,
But the cornered weasel stands his ground,   15
Shrieks at the dogs and boys set round,
Shrieks as he knows they stand all round,
And hard as winter dies.

SONNET

Rupert Brooke (1887–1915)

I said I splendidly loved you; it's not true.
  Such long swift tides stir not a land-locked sea.
On gods or fools the high risk falls—on you—
  The clean clear bitter-sweet that's not for me.
Love soars from earth to ecstasies unwist.   5
  Love is flung Lucifer-like from Heaven to Hell.
But—there are wanderers in the middle mist,
  Who cry for shadows, clutch, and cannot tell
Whether they love at all, or, loving, whom:
  An old song's lady, a fool in fancy dress,   10
Or phantoms, or their own face on the gloom;
  For love of Love, or from heart's loneliness.
Pleasure's not theirs, nor pain. They doubt, and sigh,
  And do not love at all. Of these am I.

HAIKU

There is a poetic simplicity in the Japanese haiku that cannot be reproduced in English, Japanese is a syllabic language, and a haiku is a seventeen syllable poem written with seventeen Japanese characters vertically on a scroll, usually with a stylised landscape painted beside them. The convention in English is to set out a haiku in three lines of 5 syllables, 7 syllables and 5 syllables – though many translations do not follow this formula rigidly.

The essence of a haiku is *kiro* (cutting) which means the juxtaposition of two ideas – a similar concept to *parataxis*. One of the ideas is often a *kigo*, or seasonal indicator.

Have a look at the following selection of tradition and modern English haiku and see how far they fit the criteria listed above. Then try to write your own haiku. Finally, consider the influence of haiku on Pound's concept of Imagism, in particular, *In a Station of the Metro*.

From time to time
The clouds give rest
To the moon-beholders.
  Basho

O faded flowers
You also
Are cast aside.
  Aito

My arms encircling
The equator of your waist:
The world in my arms.
  Aito

Blowing from the west
Fallen leaves gather
In the east.
  Yosa Buson

My life –
How much more of it remains?
The day is brief.
  Masaoka Shiki

Toward those stunted trees
We saw a hawk descending
On a day in spring.
  Masaoka Shiki

Don't dress up for it,
The moonlight will glamourize
Those workaday rags*.
  Chiyo

Slender fingertips
Stroking the silken lute strings –
I wish it were me!
  Chao Luan-luan

Poetry distilled
In seventeen syllables,
This is haiku.
  Kit Brewster

Haiku and guitar,
From seventeen syllables
Or six strings – so much!
  Kit Brewster

Bird? No bird would fly
A zig-zag on vampire wings
To haunt the night sky.
  Kit Brewster

Haiku are icebergs:
Three lines floating on the page,
The rest unwritten.
  Arthur Roberts

True haiku? I know
They're not very Japanese –
Nor is my language.
  Anne Harlowe

ABOUT THE AUTHOR

The basic bio can be found on the back cover – this gives a glimpse of the "inside story". I, like Pound, aspired to be a poet, but lacking his talent, did the next best thing, which was to become an English teacher. This extract from a poem in praise of Marilyn Monroe gives an idea of my poetic "manifesto":

To become a sort of poet-Monroe by writing
Poems which bring to prosody and grammar
Some of your sex-appeal and glamour,
Poems with imagery as exciting
As your see-through ballgown in *Some Like it Hot.*

I didn't make it as a "poet-Monroe" – but the field is wide open for someone who can. T. S. Eliot, Ezra Pound, and W. B. Yeats are the great poets of the 20th century – the world still awaits their equivalents for the 21st.

Chris Webster
Singapore
2016

31895972R00077

Printed in Great Britain
by Amazon